happened on the way
to chemo

A funny thing
happened on the way
to chemo

A rather unusual memoir

ILEANA VON HIRSCH

Published in 2018 by Short Books, Unit 316, ScreenWorks,
22 Highbury Grove, London, N5 2ER

10 9 8 7 6 5 4 3 2 1

A CIP catalogue record for this book is available from
the British Library.

ISBN: 978-1-78072-353-2

Cover design by Two Associates, based on an
original idea by the author

Printed at CPI Group (UK) Ltd, Croydon, CR0 4YY

———————

This book is intended to be a light-hearted take on my own experiences, designed
to provide a little guidance and support for anyone going through something similar.
Nothing in the book is intended as or should be relied upon as medical or nutritional
advice. If you have any medical conditions or doubts about your health, you
should contact a qualified medical professional.

To Florian, Danae, Conti and Tassilo

Contents

PART ONE – The Journey

An inspector calls
Chemo-brain
Chemo-glow
Cancer and the menopause, or the chemopause
Post-chemo tips
Manopause
The gynaecologist
Personal training and the gym
Cancer and TV
Cancer and work
Cancer and airports
Married bliss
Chemo-meno-insomnia
Online shopping
Cancer and social media
Me and Angelina Jolie
Cancer and Chinese calligraphy: "strong but wrong"
Chemo-sight
Small treats
Things not to say to a cancer patient
Things you can say to someone with cancer
Surgery
Anaesthetists
In hospital
Post-surgery
Radiotherapy
Faith, hope and innumeracy
Convalescence
Honey, I shrunk the tumour
The dentist

Foreword

Cancer is not a laughing matter, as I was told by a cross German lady from Dortmund when I showed her this journal. She herself had had breast cancer and is right of course; there is nothing funny about the macroscopic picture, and yet, if you put it under the microscope and focus on those little wriggling, squirming moments, there is plenty of amusement to be found. Science in fact encourages us to do so: Harvard's recent eight-year study of sick women, optimism and its effects on their health reported that women with the cheeriest life view had a 30% lower risk of dying from their disease than the least optimistic women. Its project report for 2015 found that the secret to happiness is to choose to be happy with whatever you do, strengthen your closest relationships and take care of yourself physically and emotionally. I am not really sure how they could possibly have found the opposite to be true; I mean, imagine a fully-funded study which after eight years concludes happiness does *not* consist of being happy with what one does, having close relationships or looking after one's emotional or physical health. Perhaps I missed something. Anyway, eight-year Harvard studies are not to be sneezed at and so this journal is about applying their carefully researched conclusions – which everyone knew anyway – to a less obvious scenario.

I started writing this journal as a way to entertain myself and a few friends while I was dealing with a not very remarkable breast cancer. The idea developed when a well-meaning lady sent me a book by someone who had suffered a very aggressive cancer and survived, though she had had a gruelling time of it. There are lots of things that are not fun about cancer, most of them unavoidable, but at the top of my list is something that is luckily very avoidable: namely, 95% of the books written by people who have had cancer, which all end up making you feel utterly depressed. To quote Dorothy Parker, these are not books to be put aside lightly, but should be thrown away with great force. This particular book was so horrific that I felt the need to exorcise any traces of it in my memory by writing its absolute antithesis: a *Cancer for Cowards*, a *Carry on up Harley Street*, so to speak. This is the anti-misery memoir that is safe to give to cancer patients who want cheering up, as I did, not bringing down.

I should say at this point that I am not a brave person. Quite the opposite. I am afraid of crowds and daddy-long-legs, I hyperventilate at loud noises, at lift doors not opening or trains stopping in tunnels. If people shout, I feel faint. Getting lost triggers a full-blown panic attack. Fireworks must be watched from a safe space, I keep my distance from large dogs and won't swim in muddy ponds or in the sea when there are big waves. Rock climbing and funfairs are out as I am scared of heights. In fact, I can only tolerate the absolute minimum amount of adrenaline needed to stay alive. I was therefore as surprised as the next person to realise that a huge number of funny things happen on the way to chemo, or indeed on the way to most places, and that once you get your eye in, you completely forget to be scared.

They say that if you have to get something, breast cancer is usually the thing to get – so it is easier for me to treat it all as a romp in the shallows than it is for those facing the tide going out. But breast cancer is also the commonest cancer in the UK by far, so there are many people in my position. I have friends who have gone through cancer without telling anyone, not even their family. They feel that the burden shouldn't be shared, or they can't face bringing the monster out from the shadows. I believe that to de-fang the monster can only be a good thing, and that laughter is the best de-fanger known to man. My oncologist told me that, if on the first appointment he can get someone to smile – and curiously enough, there is no correlation between the gravity of a diagnosis and the likelihood of someone smiling – then they will have an easier time of it. If a fundamentally cowardly person like me, who hyperventilates when a lift stops, can find things to smile about, then there is hope for everyone.

PART ONE

The Journey

Setting out for Ithaca,
You should hope that your journey is a long one,
full of adventures, full of experiences,
Monsters and giants,
angry gods from the depths—don't be frightened of any of
    them:
you won't ever encounter them on your odyssey
if you keep your thoughts and spirits high.

(from CP Cavafy's *Ithaca*, my own loose translation)

MANY PEOPLE LIKE TO describe cancer as a "journey". This is embarrassingly trite, but the analogy can be pushed further into more interesting territory. Cancer – or any illness – is more than a journey: it is an exploration of a new country, a *terra incognita* where the maps are still decorated with fuzzy borders and have *Here be dragons* scrawled across them. I am privileged enough to be on a very relaxing five-star escorted excursion to this continent, and I have met some of the wonderful people who live here, work here, commute or have weekend houses, but, and this is a large *but*, I then imagine I will board my cruise ship after the excursion, and sail on. Well, that is the plan anyway.

In my other life, I work in the travel world and write a blog about my travels in the Greek islands. In those little pieces, I have tried, over the years, to communicate the sheer joy and fun of exploring new and wonderful places – the people, the snatches of conversation, the food, the landscape – and these notes about cancer are the same: an extension of my travels, prospecting for gold in an unpromising little corner of the world.

Cancer is not a country which people set out to visit, but if you find yourself suddenly dumped onto its shore, take a deep breath and set out to explore your new home. There are beauties, mysteries and amusements to be had. Go for a wander along the sand, picking out the shells, corals and driftwood, following the tracks of the birds and trying to catch the scuttling crabs. You could meet some interesting fellow travellers and pick up some souvenirs. Before you know it, your ship could appear on the horizon, and you might even feel a pang of separation when the ship's tender arrives to pick you up, and the shore of the country you never chose to visit in the first place recedes and then vanishes. If your ship doesn't show any signs of coming, or persists in anchoring nearby, then at least you have squeezed everything you can out of your involuntary travels and had the best time you could have had under the circumstances.

Diagnosis

I was diagnosed in June 2016 with breast cancer, stage 3, a very late catch. The lump had to get to spectacular dimensions and spread to various lymph nodes before it was noticed as I was always too busy to do the annual mammograms that I should have had done, given that breast cancer runs in my family. It turns out that skipping mammograms is a highly inefficient way of optimising your time.

Chronologically, BC and AD still work – BC is Before Cancer, AD is After Diagnosis. Life does seem to separate into these two expanses, like the Red Sea before Moses. Life before cancer and life after.

My Moses moment happened while I was on holiday on the small Greek island of Ithaca, where my family come from. The island that inspired Cavafy's poem, it has been associated with dangerous journeys for 3,000 years. When my breast turned a bit hard and red, the local doctor didn't believe my 57-year-old self's auto-diagnosis of mastitis – "At your age? Are you mad?" – and promptly told me to get a scan done. The clinic was a pop-up affair: the scanning machine, together with a trigger-happy radiologist, came over from the neighbouring island once every two weeks, the machine held together with duct tape and Blu Tack, the doctor held together with nicotine patches. The loo was as usual out of order, and the veranda was full of old ladies with arthritis and bunions and shaky old men with dribbling bits. Everyone knew everyone – it is a small island – and patient privacy is not a concept.

"Oh, look who is here, wonder what's wrong with her?"

"I don't know, but you are treading on my bunion, move your foot."

Or, "Last time I was here the doctor said you were not taking your medicine."

"Well I am now, and I wondered when you were going to see the doctor about *your* little problem as well."

"Hello Dimitri, you are looking better this week, are you finally doing what the doctor said?" and so on.

By the time my turn came to be scanned, the radiologist was onto his last nicotine patch, and was reaching for his cigarettes. He was visibly bored, and had given up all hope of anything exciting happening beyond bunions and arthritis. He scanned me with a weary look on his face, then suddenly sat bolt upright and said, "Holy Mother of God!"

One doesn't really like providing excitement for doctors, so I asked what the matter was. He looked at me with shining eyes and said, "It is either nothing, or a very rare cancer and you have two to five years to live. Please do let me know how you get on, I don't often ask patients, but this is exciting!" I thought I had just got a touch of mastitis, so, slightly shell-shocked, I walked home slowly along the waterfront, thinking elegiac things. "How poetic: in the island of my ancestors I was given life, and now I learn I am coming to the end of it." A wave of peace and acceptance gently washed over me, the village never looked lovelier, and I suddenly saw how beautiful and wonderful everything was.

I popped into our family chemist, who is an old friend of mine. In the days when my father was alive, the chemist used to keep a bottle of brandy in the back of the shop, "for medicinal purposes" and a chat. He let me cry on his shoulder a bit, then said that, sadly, he only had rubbing alcohol now, which he wouldn't recommend. So, I dried my tears and got a lift on the back of the motorbike of a passing shepherd. He took me as far as where the asphalt gave way to earth and stones and goat droppings, from which point I walked peacefully home. I told my children that I had an abscess and I needed to go home to London to get it drained, and then I booked the next available flight back.

News goes around fast on a small Greek island. I went to the village the next day to do some errands, and like a row of Swiss weather barometers where either Herr or Frau pops out according to whether rain or sun is due, people emerged from the shops and taverna doorways to shout at me, "Are you still here? Go home and get yourself checked out."

The surgeon

A week later, back in London, my new surgeon sat with a heap of reports of all the biopsies, etc., and read through the sun-tan oil-stained, handwritten notes in Greek that I had brought him. Luckily most medical terms in English are Greek anyway, so while I painstakingly translated *polykistiki morphoma* to him as "a sort of shape thing with lots of bits in it", Mr G nodded and said, "Yes, polycystic morphology".

Then he took off his glasses and said in a serious way, "I am afraid it is cancer."

Consultants and surgeons come in all shapes and sizes, their rooms can be wood-panelled with leather desks, or plate-glass, chrome and white with orchids, but the words are the same.

"Yes," I said, "I know that already, but have I got two or five years to live?"

A look of puzzlement crossed his face. "Why would you think you only had two to five years to live?" So, I told him. He continued to look puzzled, and said, "I would say it is a perfectly normal, very treatable breast cancer. You have a 70–80% chance of surviving, and I see this sort of thing every day. In fact, I see hundreds of people like you every month."

This is the one time in your life when you should be pleased to be told that you are dead common and there are hundreds of people like you, but it still smarted a tiny bit – after all, he had only just met me. However, being told you have a boringly normal cancer after thinking you have only a few years to live is excellent news, so, whatever else Mr G said to me that day, I just remember the huge grin that kept spreading over my face, and nodding happily and saying, "That's wonderful news, thank you!" – and it was. I had been given the best possible start to my cancer journey by that trigger-happy Greek ultrasound doctor. But I am sure Mr G felt that I was a bit of a half-wit.

Mr G is a very serious Malaysian of Chinese origin. His rooms are hung with autographed photos of famous breasts.

He wears a perpetual look of worry. One wants surgeons to be serious, but I couldn't help saying, as we said goodbye after the first appointment, "Mr G, don't look so sad, please smile, it will all be fine!"

The next time I saw him was in hospital where he came to see me before inserting my chemo port – a minor surgery and well worth doing. He was wearing a slightly alarming rictus grin that made me feel a bit scared, as if he had some very bad news to tell me. Bracing myself, I asked him if there was anything wrong. "No," he replied, looking hurt, "you told me to smile more often, so I am smiling." Baby steps…

The oncologist

Oncologists are the new gods in your life. Choose your god and worship. My new oncologist, Professor E, confirmed everything Mr G had said, going through the same routine, right down to the 70–80% statistic and diagnosis of a treatable, if eye-wateringly large lump. At the end of my hour with him, he said to me gently, "You do realise that cancer is serious and life threatening, don't you, and that even if we have a good chance of treating it, there are no guarantees, because it seems to me that you really are at the extreme end of the chill spectrum and perhaps you haven't understood. Would you like an appointment with one of the nurses to go over everything with you again and help you through any shock or denial issues?"

I explained that the reason I was so chilled was the huge improvement from my initial prognosis and that I was therefore likely to remain at the extreme end of the chill spectrum. I suspected he thought I had some brain cells missing and would probably want to scan that at some point, but there we are. In my view, they are not brain cells I need to have.

My friend Linda, who is a cancer-fighting veteran of 12 years and is still having treatment, couldn't understand why her doctors refused to join in her banter at appointments. Her daughter, who is a doctor herself, told her that, unless the patient cries, you can't be sure that they have taken in the news and understood. Linda is not a crier, at least not on cue, and sees it as her personal challenge to make her doctors laugh. Twelve years on, she can count the times on one hand when she has succeeded.

I am lucky because my chosen god, Prof E, always likes to keep it fun and chatty. At one of my appointments he told me that he was off to a Breast Cancer Convention in San Antonio, Texas. I said I hoped the title was "Keeping Abreast" and what fun that would be to go to. He told me that San Antonio is the third most popular destination in the USA for US tourists. "What is there to do there?" my sister asked curiously. (She is also in the travel world, had cancer before me, and came to various appointments with me to make sure I was paying attention.)

"Absolutely nothing," he said. "I can't think why they go there, but it is a very good conference."

Perhaps I would be a case study at the conference – after all, I started to notice that, during my appointments with him, he tended to say "fascinating" whenever I said anything, and then scribbled notes on my records. Or perhaps he was also writing a book: *Funny People that*

Appear in my Consulting Rooms on their Way from Chemo. We stare into the barrels of each other's pens like a showdown in a Western. Who will draw first…?

A useful tip here: your consultant's and surgeon's secretaries are incredibly knowledgeable and very important people who control access to your oncologist and surgeon, control their lives, your appointments, your life, control the world, in fact. Do not mess with them. Ever. Give them flowers and Christmas presents and always thank them profusely for everything and anything. At the other end of the people spectrum are radiologists, pathologists, etc. They got brilliant grades at med school but prefer computer screens to people. Don't worry about small talk. Say hello, thank you, goodbye and leave.

The brain is not as smart as it thinks it is, and other coping techniques

Most of the things that occupy my mind or amuse me are things that have to do with being a woman – and are very frivolous. Even when facing the big issues, paradoxically, life gets reduced to a very small scale – achieving small goals, tempering ambition, dealing with the small indignities that treatment inflicts on you. So, in this reduced and miniature life, how does one find funny things to laugh at? Well, here are some good tips on how to make your oncologist, and others, think you too have brain cells missing, and some easy techniques that anyone can practise:

Smile

Even if you are anxiously sitting in a clinic dressing-gown with a cannula in your arm waiting for a PET/CT scan, just plaster a phony smile on your face – preferably when no one is looking, as it might take a few goes to get it right. Something very strange and marvellous happens. The brain thinks you are having a good time and joins in, and you suddenly feel that, actually, something is quite funny after all, that you need to smile a bit more, and you might even laugh out loud – which makes people look at you in a funny way, but you have cancer, so who really cares.

The pregnancy trick

An involuntary trick of the mind that I found curiously pleasant was that I went into every scan and test with the feeling that I was pregnant. There are many parallels: a lump is growing inside you, it is being measured, you are warned about feeling sick, told to get lots of rest, lay off the alcohol and eat healthily. You get to see a picture of the lump on the screen in a process which involves someone smearing cold gel over you, rubbing a sensor on top, and then giving you a completely non-absorbent bit of kitchen paper to clean yourself up with, so that you remain sticky for the rest of the day. You hug your little secret to yourself until you know what is going on and your family are all on board, and in approximately nine months' time, the lump will be gone – one way or another. The main difference, as a friend pointed out once I mentioned this strange feeling, is that at the end, rather than you rushing to put its name down for a top school and putting your flat on the market to move to a bigger house or a better school catchment area, the nurse throws the lump (or even breast if you are unlucky) away.* So much easier.

I did at one point ask Prof E what the lump looked like, and if I could keep it once it was taken out, as a memento, I suppose a sort of maternal displacement reaction. "Fascinating," he said, scribbling some more notes onto my records, "in my 25 years of being in practice, no one has ever asked me that before. In fact, since you ask, it looks like a piece of good-quality, gristly steak," adding, "I hope you aren't squeamish." I had to laugh and told him – typical man – that after you have given birth to three babies, you cannot possibly think that a small piece of steak with gristle coming out of you is going to make any impression whatsoever.

No victims please

Do not call yourself a "Cancer Victim" – you are still alive; a victim is someone who has lost a fight. It is the state of mind of someone who has given up… I imagine my cancer as lots of microscopic Jack Russells in my body – small, disobedient, invasive and with a tendency to stray, but manageable if you have a firm hand and smack them frequently on the snout. Hence the need for PET scans, perhaps. The main point is that no one would ever think of themselves as a Jack Russell victim. If you must think of yourself as something, the closest would be a sort of hairless ethnic minority.

I say Jack Russell advisedly as I spend an inordinate

---

* As Mr G told me rather crossly, of course they don't throw it away, it gets sent for biopsies and full histology reports. They don't throw ANY-THING away that they cut out of you.

amount of time trying to stop my real Jack Russell from escaping into the wider neighbourhood to go visiting/chase foxes/scavenge, which she does about three times a week – and no matter how strong our defences are, there is always a hole that she finds. I dread the telephone call that starts, "Hello? Have you lost a little brown and white doggie?" Which then means that I have to drive around as if I am a personal chauffeur service to pick her up from wherever it is she has been – neighbour, rugby club, vet, clinic, police pound, nice couple who have given her treats and prime position on their sofa, indignant animal lovers who think we are irresponsible owners. My pleas of "Pleeeeease don't be nice to her, she will come around every day, just throw a shoe at her and tell her to go home" are met with horror. And, as she is usually covered with blood (the fox's), this often means I get a call the next day from the Brent Council Animal Welfare Department to say I have been reported for animal cruelty. Straying cancer cells hold few terrors for the owner of a Jack Russell.

Choose your narrative
It is amazing how different people will take different things out of any meeting. Florian, my husband, and two of our three children are deeply mistrustful human beings who don't believe a word I say, so they insisted on accompanying me to the first oncologist's appointment to make sure I wasn't going to tell them a whole heap of soothing nonsense. After the meeting, the two mistrustful children and husband looked devastated and tearful, while I was all smiles. "Mummy," said my daughter Danaë forlornly, "you might die…"

I looked at her in total surprise. "No, no! That is not what he said at all. He said there are no guarantees but it looks perfectly treatable, and he is not worried in the slightest."

My older son, the trustful one, who had stayed at home, just asked me if I was going to be alright.

"Yes," I said.

His eyes stopped glistening, and his next communication an hour later was, "When is supper?"

By insisting on the right narrative, you can swing the general mood round to your way of thinking and then everyone feels a lot better and stops going around with welling eyes and whispered conversations when they think you are not looking. Life then goes back to normal – at least to the extent that you wish it to. Beyond this is the matter of how to exploit the unique situation you find yourself in, when life does not have to be normal – *it can, in some respects, be better.*

Avoid listening to other people

I was at the very beginning of my "journey", sitting nervously in the waiting room of the clinic where I was going to have my first scans. I had foolishly decided to go alone and was regretting it.

The day had started badly. The basement of the building had flooded and all the machines were being moved to dry land. Patients were wandering around like lost souls in open-backed hospital gowns with shower-caps on their heads, pulling behind them their belongings in red plastic shopping trolleys. Everyone was searching for something: the mechanics were looking for the machines, the electricians were looking for the mechanics, the management was looking for the electricians, the nurses were looking for the patients, the patients were looking for anyone who could tell them where they should be and what was happening. It felt like I was in the sort of contemporary drama where actors shuffle around in a sealed environment from which there is no exit, while the occasional black-suited "figure of authority" strides across the stage. The sort of play that ends in a stunned silence, then depressed and half-hearted applause, allowing the audience of 15 – comprised of out-of-work actors, relatives of the director and people who thought they were going to see a stand-up comedian – to slink out to get a stiff drink across the road.

In the reception, limbo to this hell, was a large and very noisy extended family, accompanying a middle-aged man in a wheelchair who had some horrible lung disease – from smoking too many cigarettes, according to the comments of his family. He was clearly quite at home there, an old hand, who liked a bit of an audience, and he was announcing loudly to the world in general about how he had such claustrophobia that he had panic attacks each time he had a scan, and how awful it was, and how frightening and how loud, and how the whole family had to escort him as otherwise he would duck out of the scans. "You go in 'ead first, into this machine, then all these clanking sounds start. Blimey, you would think the effing world was about to end. Then I 'av to move as I am panicking and wanna get out, and then it's all ruined, and I 'av to come in again the next week and do it all over again." He laughed so much that he had a coughing fit that sounded as if it would finish him off on the spot.

"That's right," chorused the extended family cheerfully, once he had started breathing again.

Even plastering on a fake smile was not going to help me here. I was frankly terrified, and – in an upstairs, empty waiting room where someone then plonked me, and left me alone for almost an hour with the cannula in my arm, no one in sight, no prospect of anyone noticing that I had been forgotten, perhaps for ever – I began to panic, and started looking for a way out. But all I could see were 25 doors decorated with pictures of skulls and crossbones, and signs saying "RADIOACTIVE, DANGER, DO NOT ENTER." In the end, I found a lift which took me back down to reception. I burst into the room in my shower cap and hospital gown, with a needle sticking out of my arm and trailing a red plastic shopping trolley, like an escapee from a lunatic asylum, wailing that I had been abandoned. I was instantly smothered by the receptionist there before I could frighten off any new or flight-risk patients who were waiting. I was satisfied to see out of the corner of my eye, while being bundled off, that Lung Disease Man had stopped talking and was looking horrified; serves him right.

I was then allotted a private attendant (a.k.a. security guard) to sit with me till my turn came. The moral of this story is: do whatever it takes to get attention if you feel you need it and, if you are scared, tell someone so they can help you.

When my turn finally came, I tearfully confided to the nurse that apart from all the other upsets, Lung Disease Man had scared me witless with his tales of scanning nightmares. "Him?" she exclaimed scornfully. "You don't want to pay any attention to him. I haven't been able to get him anywhere near the machine for months." She slid me calmly into the machine and there was no problem at all.

Eine kleine Scanningmusik

I say there was no problem… Well, there is one really, which hits indecisive Libras like me particularly hard. To distract you from the loud clanking noises while you are in the MRI machine, you are given a pair of headphones through which you can listen to music. The nurse asks you, "What sort of music would you like to hear? You can have ANYTHING you want. We can stream it, YouTube it, play it from your own iPhone, radio, anything you like."

This is enough to give anyone a panic attack. How do I know what I will want to hear for 45 minutes while in a loudly clanking machine? If I say classical and they choose Elgar, I am sunk, I might even have to do a Lung Disease Man. If I say Mozart but the sound quality is poor and the clanking interrupts my favourite parts, that would also be terrible. I was so wrung with doubt and dithering, that I was about to cry again. The nurse finally gave up waiting for me to decide and put Magic FM on the radio, which was, in the end, perfect, as listening to jingles about window-cleaning and competitions where you can win £1,000 for guessing a dog's name, interspersed with the Carpenters and the Bee Gees, is just distracting enough, while not so exciting that you mind missing the vital parts during the clanking. In fact, had I planned it right, I could have put in a request: "Dear Magic FM, I am going to be in an MRI today at 11.30 and would love it if you could play me a selection of your adverts and possibly the song I hate most in the world, *Dance with my Father* by Lionel Ritchie, which will make me glad of the clanking sounds from the machine. Thank you."

I have plenty of scans ahead of me over the next few years, so I might still do that.

Google

Just don't. Either someone is trying to scare you into buying something, or someone has – or thinks you have – the IQ of a beanbag. Unless a fellow cancerian has recommended an especially useful website to you, avoid them all. Chat rooms and forums are particularly dangerous places as, while they can provide some useful information, they are heavily weighted in favour of those who have horror stories to tell – of their symptoms that reached acute levels of pain and lasted ten times longer than any doctor could imagine – leaving you gaping in disbelief. If you can discipline yourself to zoom in on the specific piece of information you wanted without reading on, then fine. Otherwise, best avoid.

I did find one online forum rather useful: it was called www.we-are-not-finding-it-too-bad-at-all-in-fact-it-has-been-surprisingly-easy-thank-you.com or something similar, and consisted of cheerful women exchanging handy tips. One lady had rather misunderstood the ethic of this group and had contributed a jarringly dramatic post detailing the traumatic side-effects of a particular drug, to which the crisp response was: "Don't forget, the main side-effect of the treatment is staying alive."

A friend of mine told me how her father was Googling his symptoms and came up with an awful diagnosis with pretty appalling prospects and very unpleasant treatment.

He fretted over this for days before sending the link to his daughter, who was able to point out to him the section he had skimmed over that read: "While this is common enough in the mouth, a few horses will also display symptoms in their ears. The good news is that it rarely affects their hooves."

Enough about me, let's talk about what YOU think of me

Let's face it, in normal life, when people ask how you are, they really don't want to know. When you have cancer, you get asked all the time by brilliant and highly trained people how you are, and they *really, really* want to know. Every cough and sniffle, every hangnail, every stiff neck, every tiny fever, every headache, they hang on your every word and take notes of everything you say. You are positively encouraged to ring up an emergency number every time you sneeze, day or night, 24/7 – there was a special hotline, via a Canadian call centre in my case – and you get given goody-bags filled with miraculous drugs whenever you go for treatment: sleeping pills, anti-nausea, anti-allergy, anti-hangnails, anti-stiff neck, you name it, it's in the bag. You are a VIP, the most precious thing in the world, and everyone listens to you go on and on about anything you want. This is of course totally addictive, and I know I am going to find it hard to re-adjust when it is all over, and people will ask me how I am. I will launch into my catalogue of finely observed complaints and forget that they really are not interested.

If, like me, you spend quite a large part of every day muttering "moron" or "cretin" under your breath, then being surrounded by highly skilled and experienced professionals is like a luxury holiday for the brain. There is also something immensely satisfactory in being able to say "my oncologist", or "my surgeon", or "my radiotherapist", while others must make do with "my personal trainer", or "my manicurist", or "my nutritionist". You learn to work these very elitist possessions into all sorts of conversations, such as: "My surgeon says I should only use face-cream with low sulphates", or "My oncologist says that I should keep aspirin in the cupboard", "My radiotherapist says that June should be fine." Everyone nods solemnly and thinks you are quite splendid. More interestingly, though, since you have joined the cancer club – and its members are everywhere, scattered in among the ordinary people – trigger words like "my oncologist" can elicit some wonderful stories, and create real bonds with people you might not otherwise talk to.

Other cancers (it is not always about me...)

At a certain point, though, hard as it is to believe, you will find that other people are more important than you. This is because there is a strict hierarchy on Planet Cancer. Debrett's could publish a reference book on the order of nobility, titles, precedence and modes of address. In fact, there is as much protocol to be learned and observed as in a Japanese corporation.

Cancer patients are divided into species by their oncologists – we are known as Gynies, Bowels and Colons,

Breasts, Pancreases, Prostates, Stomachs, Brains and Lungs, Rares, Sarcomas, Heps (liver) and Hims (blood, immune system and something else). Actually it could be Haems (pronounced Heems), short for Haematology, but my main informant is a Kiwi and the way she says it is "Hims".

One day the clinic was particularly full and I asked what was going on. "Oh, we have all the Colons in today as their consultant has been on holiday." I started imagining the appropriate collective nouns to describe such mass migrations – a stampede of Colons, a clearing of Throats, a herd of Sarcomas, a rumble of Stomachs, a school of Brains, a battalion of Breasts, a flock of Gynies, an eruption of Prostates, a shoal of Bowels, a wheeze of Lungs, a pride of Rares, an efflorescence of Livers, a troupe of Hims (or Haems).

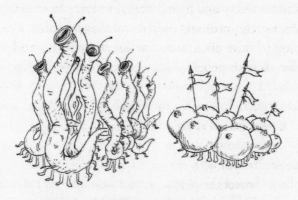

A stampede of Colons and a battalion of Breasts

Pecking order is important. Brain, Liver and Rare vie for top position, Breasts and Prostates are way down at the bottom of the heap, unless they have metastasised. Length of treatment, range of metastasis and unusual complications confer nobility and rank, while cancers that only need one treatment, single surgery or a little radiation therapy are the plebs. Stage 4 has precedence over stage 3, which in turn has precedence over stage 2 and so on. One has to know one's place.

I was sitting one day in the waiting room next to a large, cheerful lady with an air of calm authority about her. She had been on the phone to a friend and had been using with impressive fluency all the cancer-speak terms that I was still learning: histology, phlebotomists, and a whole array of unfamiliar acronyms. We started chatting.

"I am a stage 4, diagnosed in 2014," she told me, opening up with a courteous indication of her rank. I adopted a respectful position and replied that I was only stage 3.

"Ah," she said kindly, "has it metastasised?"

I admitted that it hadn't really, unless you count lymph nodes, which she clearly didn't, and then added, in a modest attempt to raise my status, that the lump had been huge.

She acknowledged that modification politely, then responded with her own modification: "I have also had neurosurgery, following metastasis to the brain, and my head is now full of titanium."

I complimented her very sincerely, remarking on how valuable she now was.

She followed this with: "And I also had necrotising jaw disease." Her final flourish was: "I am only here at a private clinic as the drug Dr C wants to try on me is not available on the NHS, which otherwise I much prefer for its camaraderie and air of ordered chaos."

This was an express lift to the top floor. Hierarchical rankings were now completely established, and I fetched her a cup of tea from the dispenser.

My friend Sara, who is an extremely high-status Rare, was interviewing a prospective new oncologist. "I suppose you are just going to give me that bog-standard chemo that is all anyone has ever offered me," she said to him as provocatively as she could, to see if he was holding back some special chemo-delicacy.

"Oh!" he said looking hurt. "It took me ten years to develop that bog-standard chemo drug and it has only been in existence for a few years. No one has anything else, I am afraid." We lowly Breasts and Prostates would never get away with that sort of thing. Respect.

Counselling

You will be offered this every two minutes. Rightly or wrongly, I happen to not want any, and said so at my first appointment with my doctor, who has known me since I was a teenager and ought to know better.

Doctor (looking compassionately at me): It is totally normal to feel anger and say, "Why me?" This is where Counselling comes in and will be very helpful.

Me: But Dr H, why *not* me? I am probably the best person on this planet to get this as I have few immediate financial worries, a nice home, grown-up children, a loving family and I'm half Jewish so have a huge supply of Jewish jokes to draw on, like the one where the whole family pees into the urine sample bottle the doctor gives them, so as to get a group health check on the cheap...

Doctor (looking worried at this, but still speaking compassionately): Well, you will at some point feel anger and ask the question, "Why me?"

Me: Never in a million years will I ask that. I have up until now hit life's jackpot, so it is hardly fair to grumble as soon as something goes slightly wrong.

Doctor (somewhat less compassionately): You don't think so now, but trust me, you will.

Me: I promise you I won't.

Doctor (glaring at me): Just take this name and number for that time when you will feel anger…

Me (holding out hand for it, as it is easier than arguing): Thank you.

While I would never say that I am glad that a friend of mine has got cancer, when my dear old friend Ben rang to say that they had just taken a tumour out of his colon, my second thought – after being assured that it was an early catch and he was in good spirits – was: oh good, Ben is totally on my wavelength. Now I have a male Colon friend to show me the male point of view, as men don't get any fun out of the small things that women do, like buying lipsticks or a new chemo hat.

I had asked a girlfriend about what men might find to lift their spirits. She thought hard for a while and then offered, "Porn?"

I asked Ben if this was the case, and he said he thought not on the whole, and promised to take notes for me. He told me that he had been offered Counselling for "When you get angry and you ask, 'why me?'" To which he had replied, "Well, why *not* me?" So we were in tune – his oncologist probably thought he had a brain cell missing too.

I once heard a rather satisfactory variation on the Counselling theme. I was telling a very brisk and down-to-earth German friend that I was secretly dreading the day I would be given the all-clear and everyone would expect me to go back to work and be the way I was BC. She snorted and said, "Their expectations are their problem, you live how you want and anyone who can't deal with it should get Counselling." It's a good thing I did take that name and number after all. You never know who might need it.

Even my family, though, are unsure whether I am just putting on a brave face. Not long ago, well after my last hair had fallen out, a friend of mine sent me one of her famous chocolate and poppy seed cakes, which of course I shouldn't eat as sugar is not part of the cancer-busting diet – but the thought was lovely and I ate it anyway in case you are interested. She sent it in a box that had a picture of its original contents on it, which had been a large, state-of-the-art German hair dryer. My daughter gave me funny looks all day, until the evening when I brought out the cake, explaining that Helga had sent it all the way from Munich.

"Mummy, was that what was in the box with the hair-dryer picture?"

"Yes," I said.

My daughter heaved a sigh of relief, "Thank God, I was about to tell Daddy that you are really having bad denial issues and needed to see someone professionally."

I am quite sure that the time I will need Counselling is when I no longer have the right to feel like a special, inspiring, brave VIP, and will be treated like a perfectly normal person again.

Your family will step up

Early on, I overheard my husband call a family conference. "Right, everyone, we are no longer in cruise mode,
we are now in crisis-control mode, so pay attention." Three
adult children, three dogs, a sister or two and our lodger
all looked at him expectantly. "This means," he announced
solemnly, "that when you have finished eating, you each
clear your own dishes, which means, you don't just leave
them near the dishwasher, *you put them in the dishwasher.*"

I am at risk of becoming so spoilt that they will always
have to put their dishes in the dishwasher from now on.

Clearing up after the three dogs is also now taboo for
me as it is unhygienic, so the family have taken that on.
Yesterday, my daughter came into the living-room and said
accusingly, "Someone has thrown up on the carpet!"

The dogs and I exchanged a look. "It wasn't me!" I said
quickly, before the dogs could get a word in. They slunk out,
tails between their legs, and my daughter quietly cleaned it
up. Perhaps she didn't believe me.

After diagnosis, your children will become more sensitive
and observant. My 27-year-old, trustful son, while not
strictly speaking on the autistic spectrum, is not known for
paying attention to the world around him, or the people in
it. I was pointing out to him how much more he seemed to
notice things since I had been diagnosed, but possibly more
significantly, since he had a new girlfriend.

Son: Not true, I notice lots of things.

Me: Like what?

Someone threw up on the carpet…

Son: Like when you change your hairstyle.
Me: Darling, I haven't had any hair for three months now…
Son: Oh. Well, you know what I mean.

Exams and other testing times

I was a real little swot at school, highly competitive, always lived for the end of term when our grades would be read out in front of the whole school, which, as I was too small for sports, was my time to shine. School reports and exams were my favourite things in the world. I didn't realise how much I missed this till I got my first oncologist's letter: "Ileana has made remarkable progress and is coping superbly with the course. Her test results are exemplary. She also sets a good example in class, being kind and helpful to both fellow students and teachers." Well, not the last sentence, but all the rest.

Only, I have no parents to show it to anymore, so, bursting with pride, I showed it to my children. "God, Mummy," they said, "you must have been unbearable at school."

"Yes," said my elder sister feelingly, "she was – especially at exam time. I was once sitting behind her in a French exam and asked her what something meant, and she just told me to shush and wouldn't answer."

My children stood speechless at the thought of my awfulness.

"Well, if I had got caught, I would have lost points," I said defensively. But it was no good. The wall was closed against me.

I tried to regain a little street cred by telling them how I risked getting into trouble by helping my sister hide empty bottles of wine after a dorm party and managed to convince the matron that the red stains down our white shirts were Ribena; and how I had once got half my class a detention for missing chapel because we were sitting in my bedroom instead while I taught them to chant "Na Myo Ho Reng Gi Kyo" in the lotus position (we had just visited a half-sister living in Los Angeles and that was the latest fad there) – but there was no coming back for me.

My hurt pride was only soothed by remembering the fact that my lump was MUCH bigger than my sister's, who had had the same cancer eight years ago. Not that I am competitive, I am just saying…

One week the unthinkable happened. I got a bad report. The nurse called me in to her little private room for a talk.

"You have not done very well in the red blood cells test, I am afraid," she said.

I felt rage boil up inside me. I do not fail tests, ever (apart from my driving test which I had to take four times, and my PADI scuba diving test which I didn't do for fear of failing it). Not doing very well is not a concept I am familiar with. I did go to exceptionally bad schools, so being top of the class was no great feat, but still…

The nurse saw the glint of ice in my eyes and hastily added, "It is not your fault, the course is a bit harder this week." As if that made it better.

"So," I said, putting on my sunglasses to hide the anger. "What do I have to do to improve? And, by the way," here a note of steel entered my voice, "I would like to retake the test next week."

"Well, you could try eating lots of cabbage and chicken livers, and you can come in next Friday for a retake if you feel you are better prepared."

"Better prepared" just added insult to injury. I glared at her, grabbed the Escorting Child – I was almost always allotted a mistrustful Escorting Child – and marched off in a fury.

And then, truly, God takes with one hand but gives with the other – in the window of the little Italian restaurant on the corner was the day's special menu. Cabbage soup to start, followed by chicken livers.

The next day I cleared the supermarket shelves of chicken livers, added cabbage leaves to my daily juice and soups (see "The cancer kitchen", p56) and passed my retake with flying colours.

This drive for perfection can slightly backfire: when I was told the good news that, after chemo, my giant lump had shrunk into three small ones and I would most likely be spared the full mastectomy, instead of jumping up and down and hugging Mr G, I felt a wave of disappointment and sat there feeling a failure, with my eyes welling up. "I was expecting the lump to have totally vanished," I said forlornly.

Hearing this, Mr G's expression changed from serious to surprised – he does this with a small movement of his eyebrow. "But Ileana," he said, "that is totally unrealistic, you have done extremely well to get this far, most people would be ecstatic to hear what I have just said." He does not know about my competitive spirit. So I dried my eyes and cheered up, as no one really gets A+ in this paper. But that is the price of being a perfectionist.

Hair loss, wigs and turbans

Men, I have no idea how to help you here, and you probably don't care anyway. Here is one really cool look, for which I must thank wonderful Camilla at the National Gallery who said that they wouldn't normally give permission for people to muck around with an image of one of their prize paintings (as I have done below), but added, "I have run this past our CEO and because it is such a great project we are happy to approve."

Cancer really does bring out the best in people.

Hair today, gone tomorrow

I really dislike baldness; I loathe shaved heads, buzz cuts, shiny pates, *scalps*... I told my husband when I married him that our marriage would last as long as he had hair – after that, I wasn't promising anything. He loses no opportunity to tell me from his elevated position on the high moral ground, that I am the bald one now, and he isn't leaving me.

My follically challenged male friends have also pointed out to me how superficial and lookist I am; and how perhaps I might now show a bit more compassion for them as I realise how draughty it can get around the neck and ears with no hair – and I have to admit that I do enjoy seeing them, even if their pates do gleam more than they used to in our salad days. So, in the end, losing hair sounds awful but in fact it does not have to be a big deal at all.

First, one can try the "cold cap", a contraption to freeze the hair follicles and reduce the fall-out; it sits on your head like a nasty accident you had with a giant octopus, and is not a good look, so I rejected that without even trying it.

The cold cap

The next dilemma is whether to shave it all off or let it fall out. I chose the let-it-all-fall-out option as the gentler, more natural one; I felt it was more interesting to see what happened if left alone, and I hate stubbly heads. I had fun combing out the drop-outs every evening; like grooming a moulting pet. At a critical point, Donald Trump and I had a similar comb-over. Then he won.

If you don't shave your hair off and you are a woman, you may experience Ileana's Law, which says that you might only have one long hair hanging in there, but it will always stick to your lipstick.

And, finally, there are wigs and hats and turbans, all great sources of fun and small pleasures. Trying on wigs is a real hoot. Who knew that Raquel Welch is the top wig designer and you can order wigs to look like her? I tried on platinum blonde ones (no, not right for short, dark Mediterraneans), chocolate cascades, honey-coloured pixie cuts, straight, curly, long, short… the works. I finally ordered a boring one that looked like my own hair – and never went to pick it up when it was ready because I was having so much fun with turbans. And spending so much money on them. I am now in deep hiding from London's leading wig shop who are stuck with my uncollected and unpaid-for wig.

Deep hiding from the wig shop

Ordering turbans is a brilliant mood-lifter. I went crazy. My sweet Parcelforce driver got used to seeing me every morning in my embroidered silk kimono (with a dragon on each breast – an inspired present from a cousin) and would ask, "What colour is it today?" The idea is to have a new look every morning; the colour and flamboyance can really alter how you feel. It used to be said that you could tell a woman's class by her shoes and her mood from her hat. I would go further and say that you can actually change your mood by choosing the right head covering. Turban-therapy. A bright orange turban with a gold earring ornament acts like a shot of vitamin C and coffee. A moss-coloured one with pearl earring makes you feel sophisticated and soignée. A black one with a feather clip makes you want to dance. And for bathtime… vast Sofia Loren affairs in towelling. The biggest and lushest are made by a company that sends head coverings to orthodox Jewish women who of course also have to fit the Big Hair under the turban.

One of the advantages of turbans over wigs is that they give you a visible badge of specialness. One doesn't really want to be treated like your Average Joe when one's mind is on higher things. I see it as a mark of belonging, albeit temporarily, to a more interesting tribe than other people.

Wearing a turban changes things. Middle Eastern or Muslim gentlemen react to you in a whole different way if you are a female. In general, you will notice that you are now being looked at approvingly; not lasciviously, but approvingly. The first time I wore a turban in London I was going to meet a girlfriend for lunch, and as I was waiting for her, a very nice-mannered gentleman from Kuwait invited me to sit with him and drink coffee. "You look my like my sister," he said. I put my hand on my heart and thanked him and felt most pleased with myself for the rest of the day as he was rather nice and attractive. A world of possibilities seemed to open up to me.

Shopping in a turban

I am a placid driver, but I do suffer from trolley rage when doing the supermarket shop. I want to get around there in record time and out as soon as I can. I am all stream-lined, ruthless efficiency and finely tuned but aggressive trolley-pushing. No quarter is given, not even for the elderly couples, the mothers with screaming babies in prams, the special needs groups on a weekly outing, and especially not for toddlers having tantrums. The last category gets run over. It is a great way to distract them – they stop having their tantrum, and everyone (well, possibly not their mothers) looks at you gratefully. If I ever do have Counselling, supermarket entitlement and trolley rage will be what need addressing.

My trolley rage is received rather differently when wearing a turban. I was explaining this to a friend: that shoppers look crosser than usual about being forced out of my path when I'm in my new incarnation as a turbanned, middle-aged lady. I attributed this to their latent racism/ islamophobia. "No," said my friend, "they just think you are showing off and trying to be *uber* cool in the latest fashions."

On the other hand, high street shopping becomes a joy. Waft into any store you like wearing an elegant turban and see the improvement in service. If you are an upscale

Middle Eastern cancer patient and wear sunglasses and a turban anyway, these small, new pleasures are lost on you, I am afraid, but you have had it good for a long time, so move over...

Brows and lashes

Losing eyebrows is a nuisance as it adds over five minutes to your beauty routine in the morning – one doesn't often have a steady hand with chemo, so drawing eyebrows on with a crayon is tricky. You can achieve some startling results as you make stabs at remembering where they were and getting your hand to follow your directions. I spent one year at art school with classical drawing classes and life models, and I still get unusual results.

One day, on my way to a meeting, I thought I would treat myself to a professional eyebrow session or, as we women say, "invest" in one. I went to the newly opened brow bar of one of London's department stores: acres of shiny surfaces, 25 beauticians and only one customer. They pounced on me. I explained that I needed to be shown how to draw on eyebrows, bravely mentioning chemotherapy, and an Indian girl with a perfect pair of swallowtail brows and lashes an inch long took me on. "Ah, yes, I see, I have the perfect colour for you," she said. She carefully selected a handful of pens and pencils and laid me down on the recliner. I think I got an eyebrow massage first, followed by delicate soothing strokes, like being touched with the tip of a feather. "You can look now," she said after five minutes, and I sat up – then nearly leaped out of my seat as two fat, woolly, orange caterpillars appeared to be eating their way across my face.

"Umm, I don't really think that is my colour, to be honest," I said, wondering whose colour that could possibly be. "Could we try another colour?"

"Well, there is Indian Chocolate," she said doubtfully, as if any blotchy European could presume to think they would suit a colour called Indian Chocolate, when you clearly needed a liquid caramel-coloured complexion like hers.

"Yes, let's wipe off that Sunset Glow, or whatever it is called, and try that."

She shrugged in the uninterested sort of way that says, "Well, you are paying so I will do whatever stupid thing you tell me to."

This time, when I sat up to look, the orange caterpillars looked as if they had been blasted with a flame thrower and shrivelled up and died on the spot, leaving two charred corpses. I realised that we were not on the same wavelength, so I gave her a large tip, bought all the pencils she held out to me and made my escape to the closest Ladies, where I wiped it all off and put on my sunglasses for my meeting.

Losing eyelashes – well there is nothing you can do about that, to be honest. Sunglasses are the only answer. If you also find your eyes run non-stop (a common chemo side-effect), the tears rolling down your cheeks from under the sunglasses can be fun, as people think you are a minor celebrity with a broken heart. I gave up trying to tell people I wasn't crying, and just settled for looking tragic and mysterious. Again, this can be turned to good use when in a queue or competing for a seat or anything like that. If your nose also runs – known as "chemo drip", a side-effect that highlights what nostril hairs are for (to keep mucus up your nose; an insight courtesy of Fiammetta Rocco, culture editor of the *Economist*) – then it can be less appealing, but still you can make it work for you.

The bald truth

Sometimes, hard as it is when one is in possession of 25 turbans, red lipstick and Indian Chocolate brow pencil, in all modesty, one is better off not being beautiful. There are reasons why it can be beneficial to appear visibly sick.

We have a very difficult neighbour, a successful architect who is extremely excitable, loses his temper at the drop of a hat and is, in my opinion, highly unstable. All his neighbours try to steer clear of him, and one would hope his clients do too. After enduring a particularly abusive visit from him one evening, when he complained about my dog getting into his garden and threatened that he would trash ours in response, my husband had finally had enough and called the police. The next morning, slightly chastened by having a police file opened on him for criminal damage, the architect came around to apologise. I deliberately removed my turban before answering the door, and he had to endure being lectured by a bald, in-your-face Cancer Victim, who, whenever he tried to interrupt, told him, "I have very limited resources at the moment, as you can see, so please try to control your aggressive tendencies – which seem to be a problem you have – and allow me to finish speaking."

Very childish, as my children told me when I gleefully recounted my triumph. "Mummy," said my younger son sternly, "that is grotesque, like Professor Quirrell in *Harry*

Potter unwrapping his turban to reveal that he is Lord Voldemort. And then cackling."

But, gosh, watching the angry architect squirm furiously while being totally unable to shout at me mopped up a ton of free radicals there and then.

Cold callers and other unwanted phone calls

This is where you can really have loads of fun. You know you have always secretly wanted to do this, and now you can…

Cold caller from Bangalore: Am I speaking to Mrs Bon…?

Mrs von Hirsch: Yes?

Cold caller: I would like to wish you a very good evening and ask you how you are enjoying yourself today, Ma'am?

Mrs von Hirsch: Not at all in fact, I have just been told I have cancer, and I don't feel like talking to anyone.

It works much better than putting Wagner on and placing the receiver next to the loudspeakers, which is what I normally do.

Be warned, though: this can occasionally backfire.

A sweet girl who has been trying to sell me advertising space in a magazine for a while finally caught me on the phone, and I told her I was not going to place an ad this year.

"Oh," she said. "May I ask why? Is it a question of cost? We can do something about that…"

"No," I said and, to try to cut the inevitable discussion of price and media statistics short, I added, "I have just started chemotherapy and I don't have the energy."

"Oh, I am so sorry," she cried. "I will put you on my prayer list – praying makes all the difference, you know?" And she then had me on the phone for 20 minutes while she told me that she had Parkinson's and her faith had saved her and she was still working, and about how many of her friends she had also saved through prayer. By the end, I promised to put her on my prayer list too, and had to admit that I had been most convincingly outmanoeuvred and put in my place. Parkinson's outranks breast cancer any day... I didn't buy the advertising space, though.

My younger son has recently installed a call-blocker for me, as he finds my behaviour unacceptable, so that bit of fun is sadly over – and some potential Wagnerites in Bangalore are being deprived of their opportunity to discover *The Ring Cycle*. My son can be rather a spoil-sport.

The cancer kitchen

If you have reduced your workload, as I have, you will have lots more time, and some surplus energy – and so the kitchen may well become your new field of operations. Your goal – and challenge – is to see how often you succeed in eating food which is 100% good for you and bad for your cancer cells. Forget taste and appearance. This is a whole new dimension to cooking – the old rules no longer apply. And, of course, everyone must eat willy-nilly whatever you produce because it is good for you and you have cancer.

Sadly, it seems that cancer cells and I share exactly the same taste. We love roast beef and buttered toast, we adore chocolate, we crave cookies at teatime, and we will scoop Nutella with our fingers if there is nothing else in the house (cancer cells have little tentacles that can scoop Nutella, naturally). Give us a sniff of a cake, or any sugar at all, and we break cover and push aside every other living organism to get to the feeding trough. This is how cancer cells get caught out in PET/CT scans. You have fluorescent sugar injected into your bloodstream, and the scanner picks up the greediest cells which are quickest to the sugar trough – and these are invariably cancerous. In this sense, cancer cells aren't very bright.

Cancer cells love sugar as much as I do

What this means, though, is that you have to deprive them of their (and your) favourite foods – give up all those delicious things and instead stuff yourself with broccoli and cabbage. Cancer cells hate these, just like you do. Your new goal is to see how disgusting you can make anything, on the principle that if you hate it, so does your cancer.*

Juices

Juices are a great place to start. You can get your daily dose of disgusting in one go. Buy one of those ninja machines that whizzes everything up, and experiment every day with throwing in as many bitter green leaves as you can – adding apple juice is for wimps – and see just how foul you can make the drink on a scale of one to ten. I usually get to nine – Swiss chard can be relied upon to boost the score, fast – and then add sheep's yoghurt and salt which can sometimes push it up to ten. If you are going to do the sissies' soft option with fruit juice, make sure to include the peel, core, worms, mushy bits, pips and stalks as well. If you pick the odd non-edible leaf in the garden by mistake, it doesn't matter: it just means you don't have to take the laxatives for a day or so. The funny thing is that I now find it all quite delicious. I am thinking of writing a recipe book called *Hard Core*.

Bone broth

You graduate to this from juices. The principle is the same. How many unsavoury ingredients, such as bones, knuckles, sinews, ligaments, kidneys, herbs, roots, onions, bugs and flies, etc., can you squash into your stockpot, and how long can you simmer it before the household rebels? That is the challenge. After two days, your family will be ready to move out. Your house will smell like an abattoir but, as

---

* Not based on any scientific evidence.

your sense of smell tends to go anyway, you don't really care what everyone else has to put up with.

Hard core healthy green juice

Once you have your bone broth, you can then bring your earlier-acquired juicing skills into play, and turn it into…

Soups
The technique here is to throw as many bitter green leaves, herbs, garlic cloves, spoonfuls of turmeric, cruciferous vegetables (Brussels sprouts and horrible kale), red and orange roots, stalks and stems, eyes of toad and tails of newt into your cauldron as you can – until, again, you reach ten on your disgusting scale.

Chocolate brownies
A recipe I highly recommend is a version of chocolate and beetroot brownies adapted from Christine Bailey's wonderful cookbook, *Nourish*, produced by Penny Brohn

Cancer Care (order from their really helpful website, penny-brohn.org.uk, where there is lots of good advice for cancer patients).

In Christine's recipe, beetroot replaces flour, coconut oil replaces butter and xylitol replaces sugar. You then add huge quantities of 90% cacao dark chocolate. But – and this is the vital bit – I make it extra healthy and avoid artificial anything by *leaving out the sweetener entirely.*

You then end up with a deliciously moist and crumbly brownie with a rich dark colour that is totally inedible. You will eat it all yourself, out of chef's pride, the whole nine-inch cake, and will never want to see another brownie again. I promise you this works. I haven't touched chocolate since. Well, not with the same greed as before… and my cancer cells retreated in misery.

Bokashi

One of my cousins is an eminent microbiologist and haematologist in Vancouver, with a special expertise in cancer and the blood. She moonlights as a writer for an exciting local gardening club newsletter called *The Leaf*, which she sends me to help with my chemo-induced insomnia. When I told her about my new juicing regime, she replied that she would send me something good, and I duly received this recipe which is microbiologically engineered for maximum nutrients. I had high hopes for a cutting-edge silver bullet:

She wrote:

I promised you "bokashi" using "pickling bacteria" (lactobacilli, yeasts and phototropic microbes).

You have to start it, like a yoghurt starter, by feeding

it some bran, a bacterial mix and your dinner scraps – including meat and dairy. Toss it all into an air-tight bucket, slap a lid on it to keep air out and the smells in, store in a warmish place and wait. Use a second bin in the meanwhile. Two to three weeks later have a look. The results can be dried in the sun and added to start future bokashis…

It sounded disgusting enough to be totally convincing and I made a mental note to buy two new bins. However, I read on and saw how the sentence finished:

…which can be added either to the soil, or to your compost to do wonders for your garden.

Even I draw the line at eating that.

The power smoothie
This is for when you can't eat and are losing too much weight – never my case, sadly, but for others.

I discovered this recipe when one of my children – who are all on the skinny side anyway – was going through a bad patch and had no appetite. The child was fading away before my eyes, and, no matter what I tried – and I did not shy away from emotional blackmail: "If you don't eat I will get stressed and my cancer will come back" – nada, nothing.

Finally, in desperation – as Greek-Jewish mothers take a refusal to eat as the ultimate maternal failure and the end of the world – I whizzed up whatever I had to hand that looked as if it could be fattening: avocadoes, coconut cream, agave syrup, honey, bananas, peanut butter and Nutella... and added half a kilo of some food supplement that someone had sent me called Maca (for "stressed systems").

"Yum-yum," said my child in surprise, and downed the lot.

It did occur to me that, had this failed, I would probably have tried throttling next. A re-reading of filicide stories in Greek myths is imminent: Medea's children wouldn't eat their greens and pushed all their food off their high chairs onto the floor until she just couldn't stand any more...

Medea – a Greek tragedy

Shopping for the cancer kitchen

Smugness knows no bounds at the check-out in the supermarket as you unload all the bitter green leaves, bushels of kale, quinoa and sheep's yoghurt you have been persuaded into thinking should be your staple diet. And when the friendly attendant on the till asks what you are going to do with all of that, hoping for a nice recipe tip, you tell her about your bone broth, and cruciferous green, and leafy vegetable juice – and she falls silent in sympathy for your family and wordlessly hands you the receipt and an extra token to put in the charity boxes.

Domestic hygiene

If I am being honest, my idea of domestic hygiene is having a quick look around to make sure no one is watching when I pick up a piece of fallen food off the kitchen floor and put it back on the plate. The pre-wash cycle on the dishwasher is three dogs licking the plates.

The dogs have no boundaries at all in our house. The bathtub is the only sanctuary and, even then, the Jack Russell jumped in once when I was having a soak. She didn't know that I like my baths scalding hot, so she jumped out again howling as soon as she hit the water, and she never tried it again.

On the hygiene front, my motto is, "What the eye doesn't see, the heart doesn't mind," and as I am both short- and long-sighted, and astigmatic as well, the eye really doesn't see that much at all. I bought a bottle of spray for the kitchen that "kills 100% of all known germs", but it is more of a talisman to light candles in front of, as I wouldn't know where to start spraying it.

I dream of neat, shining rows of cling-filmed steel bowls in the fridge, where strict apartheid prevails between the dairy and meat and vegetable compartments. Alas, in reality my fridge is a rainbow nation. What with having an old and dusty house, with three dogs and eight people living in it, a cleaning lady with an active mobile-phone-based social life and a general high tolerance for grime, no one has ever called my house sparkling.

I have a dearly beloved Greek cousin who has the cleanest house, husband, dogs, children, garden, kitchen floors, clothes, you name it, that I know of. Once, when we were both breastfeeding our similarly aged children, she left me to watch her baby while she went out for a bit. The minute she left, her baby opened his eyes, looked at me thoughtfully, and started howling. This of course woke my baby up who also started howling. After 20 minutes of this, I gave up and stuck a baby on each breast, and we had quiet. When I told my cousin on her return, she went pale, clutched her son tightly and rushed off muttering. Instead of being happy that her baby had been given a whole level of grime-immunity that he would otherwise not come across till his first school dances in his teens, she took him to get tested for everything from rabies to diphtheria. Such was her regard for my mastery of domestic hygiene.

So, when my oncologist said, "You know your immune system is now severely compromised, so you must always carry hand sanitiser with you, wear gloves when handling raw meat, wash your hands after touching your pets or picking things in the garden, and avoid germs and dirt in general," I tried to keep a straight face. My immune system will just have to take its chances.

In fact, the whole time I had chemo, I never had so much as a sniffle, while weaker organisms than mine went down left, right and centre with every autumn and winter bug that came along. Chemo cleared up a chronic bladder condition, a fungal infection of my toenail that I seemed to have been born with and all sorts of other annoying little things that simply got nuked along with the cancer. Cold and flu viruses took one look at the toxicity of their proposed accommodation, *chez moi*, and went elsewhere. Even a 24-hour stomach bug that I succumbed to once only lasted half an hour. In a way, I was never healthier.

Who am I?

I studied philosophy at university and have vague memories of being faced with, and dealing with, existential questions of Self and Identity. My older son, in fact, when he was about four years old, woke up one night wailing in distress, and when I tried to comfort him, he said, between sobs, "Mummy, when I go to sleep at night, how do I know I am still me when I wake up in the morning?" These questions no longer bother him, validating the old Jewish definition of a child prodigy: a child as smart at four as at 14.

I hadn't realised that the tussle of self and identity is alive and well in hospitals and clinics. When undergoing chemotherapy, from the first treatment we receive, we get a tag on our wrist with our name and date of birth, and we are asked by every person who comes near us to confirm who we think we are and when we think we were born. The nurses, with whom you have been chatting for weeks about boyfriend troubles (theirs), hot flush management (yours) and other matters, will ask you at the beginning of every chemo session what your name is in such a serious way that you are slightly afraid it is a trick question, something that you might even get *wrong*, or have to pass on. So you think very carefully then give it your best shot – one never knows with chemo-brain… and then the blessed relief when you get it right and they agree that is who you are and smile happily at you for giving the correct answer.

This continues in a particularly surreal way as they administer the chemo drugs. You begin with all the silly stuff, or "pre-meds": steroids, anti-nausea and other drugs, which get hooked up in little transparent bags to your personal trolley with no fuss at all. Then, the *pièce de résistance* arrives: a specialist nurse will appear, solemnly bearing in her arms a precious package, laid out reverentially in a special tray like baby Jesus in the manger, or the rarest of fine wines. The main drug, the transparent bag *du jour*. The specialist nurse will lean in close and ask you once more who you are and when you were born, and then, if you pass that test, she leans towards you again like the sommelier at the Ritz and whispers in tones of awe, while pointing to the label, "Epi-Rubicolitosis, specially made on the ninth of the tenth, two thousand and sixteen, expiry date the eleventh of the tenth, two thousand and sixteen."

You look at the label, check that it really says Epi-Rubicolitosis, check the dates on the label, check to see if you still are who you said you were, and then, if you are, you nod approvingly at the clarity of the liquid, and say,

"Yes, that looks delicious, please pour it." And don't even think of sending it back and saying it is corked.

I once heard someone trying to hide their age to the nurse and, as a joke, took 20 years off. The nurse wasn't having any of it. "I need you to know what year you were born please, or you won't get your Epi-Rubicolitosis."

The Tuesday Lunch Club

Chemo is the scary bit; one hears nothing but horror stories, but to be honest, it can be fun. Truly. Despite the fear-filled wait before starting, my first look at my chemo suite was love at first sight – panelled cubicles, white leather recliners, with fully adjustable foot rests, back rests, height and arm rests, consoles with buttons to call the stewardess, the clinic menu at hand, magazines and a carafe of water, a cupboard with blankets and pillows. I knew I was home.

The first time is frightening, like anything really, so have someone come with you – that way, you can pretend to be brave. After that, it becomes like brushing your teeth.

Have friends come and keep you company. When I was working, I never had time to have lunch with friends. Doing 16 chemo sessions meant that once a week, and then once every three weeks, I would have lunch while having my chemo with a friend or two. They had clinic menu smoked salmon sandwiches; I had Pachitaxol and Epirubicin with steroids as a side.

We called it the Tuesday Lunch Club and there was soon a waiting list to join. I should really have been in restaurant PR. Patients were technically only allowed two friends to lunch at a time, but the appeal of free smoked salmon sandwiches in London cannot be underestimated, so there were usually more. Meanwhile, my children vied with each other to escort me to and from my appointments.

One day, one of the nurses finally lost patience. "How can I get to you if you have an emergency when there are all these people blocking my way?" she demanded. As she is over six foot tall and very generously built, the thought of her stampeding across, through, or more likely over the lunching friends was graphic enough to make them obediently melt away to the sides of the cubicle.

I noticed over time that a curious thing happens: from the elevated position of your chemo chair, you seem to radiate calm and wisdom, tempered, as people think, in the furnace of suffering. In fact, it is just the antihistamine in your cocktail making you sleepy, but friends seem to find it easier to talk of matters that are important to them than if you were having a regular lunch. Just don't actually fall asleep unless you have a very dear friend like one of mine, who said cheerfully, "Don't worry if you feel like a nap, go ahead, and I will just keep talking." I did and she did.

The clinic pharmacist used to come around every session with her clipboard to see what drugs I needed. My dimmer guests thought she was taking orders for coffee and chocolates. I had to explain she was my dealer and all she supplied was drugs. Mark, who is an old pot-head friend of mine from student days, immediately tried to muscle in, but we know the rules.

A very cool French friend called Paula was also there for

lunch that day. She ruthlessly edited Mark's lunch order: "Coronation chicken salad, *eughhh – seulement les Anglais*." She ordered him something else.

Mark, being English, would have much preferred the coronation chicken salad, but, being English, was too polite to say anything and meekly nibbled at the smoked salmon sandwich that came instead. Paula had seen the main chemo drug being ceremoniously presented to me and the label read out like a fine *millésime*, so, being a good Frenchwoman, champagne was on her mind. She heard me tell the pharmacist–dealer taking my order that I had plenty of Domperidone (an anti-nausea pill) and didn't need any more. "*Quoi?*" she exclaimed, "Dom Perignon? *Ça alors! C'est génial en Angleterre*, you can get champagne in suppository form now on your health insurance!" The French will take anything in suppository form, of course.

Could we soon be seeing some diversification from Moët Chandon? Maybe a new investor? I await news of Pfizer Louis Vuitton Moet Hennessy – PLVMH, a small logo change, that's all...

Dom Perignon suppositories

One day, having a quiet lunch with a friend in my chemo cubicle, we became aware, from two cubicles down, of one of those mobile phone conversations – the sort that make you stop whatever you are doing and just listen. A bright female voice was recounting a long story to a friend of hers, which involved the misadventures of her 16-year-old son trying to board a cheap flight to Corfu, but who was impeded by a piece of luggage he had forgotten to check in. In the end, he had to order an Uber to take the suitcase back to West Sussex, which was going to cost more than the flight to Corfu. "Such presence of mind," cooed the voice. Somehow the suitcase ended up being thrown out of the cab on the M4 as the credit card didn't work – leaving all the suitcase contents flying around. We heard how they had to hide this from her (clearly doting) husband who already thinks – and here she put on an American accent – "Lucy, you mollycoddle those kids too much."

We had stopped our conversation with the nurses, giving up any attempt at not eavesdropping, and fell quiet, the better to hear. I wished I could meet the owner of the voice. As luck would have it, we crashed into each other wheeling our chemo trolleys to the loo. Once we had untangled ourselves, we decided there and then to become great friends. That the voice belonged to the wonderful Lucy O'Donnell – honourable exception to the misery-memoir school of cancer writing and mentor extraordinaire to so many cancer patients and their families worldwide – was a gift from God. It just goes to show that every chemo cubicle has a silver lining. As Lucy herself says, she should not really still be alive, but she is – and most delightfully so. Her book *Cancer is My Teacher* is full of good sense, compassion and tips, and gives practical advice (also found on her really good website cancerismyteacher.com), such as bringing bed socks to chemo as your feet get cold, and how to avoid people you don't want to see. She has, in fact, become, rather brilliantly, a cancer coach – to help the less experienced through the maze of orthodox and alternative options, accompanying them to appointments, where someone more *compos mentis* and alert than the typical cancer patient and their anxious family can be invaluable when it comes to asking the right questions and paying attention to the answers.

The next time we had chemo together, she brought a girlfriend along who had had breast cancer a while ago and was now all clear. We all three had the same surgeon, and the same oncologist, so started sharing notes. As the new girl with little experience, I sat quietly and listened. At one point as they discussed reconstructive surgery, they both suddenly whipped off their tops in order to illustrate their different results and compare the surgeon's handiwork (reassuringly excellent, by the way). I was in a bit of a quandary – not whipping off my top might have appeared prudish and stand-offish, but whipping it off would be getting above my station, and, especially as I had not had any surgery, a little bit exhibitionist, perhaps. We need an etiquette book for all manner of situations.

Funnily enough, I have been in a similar quandary before. I was on a villa inspection trip to the island of Skopelos, where my charming guide for the day was the eminent photographer Martin Beckett, who kindly volunteered to drive me around and show me his favourite spots. Basil, the terrier, sat in the passenger seat of his beat-up car, which is one of a series of cars that Martin has driven into the ground before throwing away. Basil was recovering from a torn cruciate ligament and didn't want to go for walkies, but the sun was hot, the sky was very blue, and Martin wanted to show me a beautiful beach. So we drove over the roads, slashed and rutted by the late summer rains of the previous week, under green glowing pine trees, down to a stunning sandy beach with blue water the same colour as lavatory cleaner. Never had a swim been more enticing. Martin looked a little shy and then confessed that he didn't have swimming trunks with him. Would I mind if he swam in the nude? Not in the slightest, I said – but I was then faced with my dilemma: I *did* have a bikini with me – I never move in Greece without one – but, if I put mine on, it might make him more embarrassed about his lack thereof. I might seem a terrible prude. If, on the other hand, I didn't put mine on, choosing to swim nude when I had a clothing option, it might make me seem like a middle-aged predator. English boarding school had not prepared me for such niceties. In the end, I compromised and just put one part of the bikini on. When I told my Greek business partner about it, she cried with laughter. "Good Lord," she said, "only the English would take off their clothes out of politeness. I clearly can't let you go on villa inspection trips on your own any more." And then she told me I ought to spend more time in Greece as I was becoming peculiar.

Chemo and zen

The zen state that chemo can induce in you – both chemically, with all the pre-meds like steroids and antihistamines, and philosophically, as you slow down and discover life from a different angle – was a welcome novelty for me, a person to whom friends politely refer as energetic. Returning home on the Underground from one chemo session with escorting daughter, whose job it was to make sure that, in my antihistamine daze, I didn't wander off and get lost, we sat next to each other and discussed dinner that evening – to which a relative with whom she had had a *contre-temps* was invited and my daughter was not comfortable about being there. Still emanating chemo wisdom and tranquillity as opposed to my usual pull-yourself-together style of advice, I gave her a few gentle and thoughtful insights as to why it would be good if she were present. I noticed that the young man sitting opposite was listening intently. Suddenly, he leaned over and said very earnestly to my daughter, "You know, your mother is quite right, you should take the higher moral ground. I have a similar situation with an aunt of mine and I always try to be the better man." They then discussed how to handle relatives, while I sat quietly and looked wise.

With your new reputation for mellowness and sagacity, this is the time to impress family, friends and colleagues with what a nice person you really are, and how badly they have misunderstood you all these years. So reach out to everyone and feel the love. It is interesting to see how my relationships with friends have changed as well: the new, gentler me, with time on her hands and a penchant for early nights and languid chat, has seen unexpected promotions and demotions in the friends' league. I hope that the wider range of qualities I now embrace and value is something that will remain with me long after hair, energy and my full vocabulary (see "Chemo-brain") have all returned. Life in slow motion reveals delicate and intimate details that those who zoom around in the fast lane never notice. I don't ever really want to pull back out into that fast lane.

Of course, chemo affects everyone differently. There are "sofa days", when even the most loving of husbands, friends, children and dogs tend to give you a wide berth. However, there is another, very important aspect to chemo which people don't appreciate, which was brought home to me by a friend who has had a tumour removed without needing further treatment of any kind. Apart from realising that he had very low status, he found that the outside world expected him to be back to normal after the usual month of recuperation from an operation – *but he wasn't back to normal.* He had had cancer, and what he really needed was time off to get his head around it and turn the ongoing anti-cancer fight into his main priority. As the world didn't see him getting chemo, he is struggling to get acknowledgement of his altered life – and he may even need Counselling.

An inspector calls

One Tuesday in the chemo suite, the normally chatty and smiling nurses and doctors were all distracted and preoccupied. I asked what was wrong and they muttered darkly about a surprise inspection which meant that none of them could get their work done, have lunch or look after us properly. I felt outraged (not that I am territorial at all) that my perfectly run piece of heaven, populated by angels in white, playing harps and dispensing drugs, advice, smiles and reassurance, was being invaded by the Dark Forces.

One of whom unguardedly approached me with a clip-board. "Would you mind answering a few questions?" she asked.

I could hardly pretend to be busy or about to rush off, hooked up as I was to my chemo trolley. I was trapped, so to speak. In revenge, I figured that I would just reply "excellent" to everything, and did so for the first 20 questions, which were all about whether I felt I was being treated with respect (yes), whether there was privacy (I was not going to let on about the delightful and total lack of privacy), whether staff answered questions, smiled, made me feel welcome, safe, blah blah blah. After hearing me rattle off "excellent" or "ten out of ten" for a while, the Dark Force became suspicious and eyed me in a cunning and not entirely pleasant way. "So, you say the communication of the various treatments available was excellent... How exactly did they communicate those treatments to you?"

I was a bit stumped, to be honest, and looked at the Dark Force in silence, trying desperately to think of an answer, as I admit I had stopped paying attention to her questions a while back... "Um, give me a minute," I said. "Chemo-brain, you know..."

The Dark Force was keen to get on, so she prompted me. "Leaflets perhaps?"

"Yes!" I agreed enthusiastically. "That's right, leaflets, lots of leaflets, all sorts, very helpful leaflets, lovely colours, really good printing, nice paper, clear pictures." She ticked the box in a satisfied way.

Then she asked, "Do you see the nurses wash their hands a lot?"

This was a tough one as there is no hand basin in sight of

the chemo cubicles, so no, we didn't see the staff wash their hands a lot. I pointed this out to the Dark Force. "Aha," she exclaimed in triumph, pleased to have found a negative, "so you would say no, you don't see them wash their hands a lot."

I wasn't having any of that. "No, I am not saying that I don't see them; I am saying I can't see any hand basins at all from where we sit, so even if they did wash their hands a lot, I wouldn't see them, so the question is a false one."

There was a standoff for a few minutes, as there was no box for that, so she then said she had better put that, yes, I did see them wash their hands a lot, as I wasn't going to say no. I said I thought that would be best. She sighed loudly, made some black marks on her page, gave me a false smile, said thank you and took her clipboard elsewhere.

There are other angels wafting around the clinic: Macmillan nurses who trail reflexologists, mindfulness mentors and meditators, and who bring with them invitations to coffee mornings, and offers of beauticians and other wonderful things. All that is missing is a mani-pedi.

I did sign up for a clinic-run beauty session, and found myself in a large room full of ladies in various stages of hormonal upset and chemo-decrepitude, all armed with free goody bags of beauty products donated by kind brands eager to introduce us to their products. A battle-hardened make-up artist who had clearly been doing this for some time presided over us and kept control, making sure we only opened the boxes we were told to in the right order and didn't fall behind or get too far ahead. More angels hovered behind us to help open boxes, as chemo can give you numb fingertips and make you clumsy.

I got far too far ahead and was caught rubbing a cream

all over my face which turned out to be a bright green complexion corrector (no, I had never heard of that before either). I was sent, green-faced in shame, to the back of the class to wash it off. I was then allowed to humbly ask the Battle-Hardened One to show me how to put on eyebrows. Even people with green faces need eyebrows. He pencilled in a very chic pair, but not before looking at the three hairs that had not yet fallen out. "Ooh," he said, tutting over them, "you should really pluck those, they are in completely the wrong place." I said that seemed to be a bit hard on them, to have survived this long and then be plucked out. I thought I would just leave them for the time being, a sort of mark of respect for war veterans, and, if I was lucky, they would just fall out too. He seemed happy with that.

Macmillan guardian angels with eyebrow pencils

Official cancer massages are a disappointment. Health & Safety and insurance companies do not like therapists to offer massages to cancer patients. One of my sisters is a trained therapist, and the official "Massage for Cancer Patients" course is really all about seeing how little you can do while still getting paid. The idea is not to get any cells too excited and end up spreading anything. While one doesn't want to get pounded to pieces, there is no need to buy 100% into all that. My friend Lucy was early for chemo one day so booked a civilian massage nearby to pass the time. When she whipped off her wig, the therapist just said, "Ooh, you do keep your hair nice and short," and gave her the full treatment, so one can try to brazen it out.

Chemo-brain

Chemo-brain is the effect that chemo can have on your memory, powers of perception and ability to home in on even the simplest word of your choice. It is rather like being mildly concussed: you can have long conversations without any reference to a proper noun or name of any kind, along the lines of "I read a fabulous book by um, you know... the one all about the um, you know what... I left it for you to read in the bathtub, I mean on the table." And so on, *ad infinitum*. If you are talking to someone else with chemo-brain, this can burble on pleasantly for hours.

Driving requires special attention as the mind does tend to wander rather. I was driving along one day when I saw a car on my side of the road coming towards me. I suddenly was no longer sure who had got it wrong, the other car or me, so I pulled over to Google on my phone "Which side of the road do we drive on in the UK?" The other car was wrong, as it happened. Perhaps that driver was also suffering from chemo-brain. The point is, though, that *I wasn't sure* and had to check.

Another day, while trying to exit a parking lot from the wrong lane, I found myself stuck on the wrong side of a barrier, nonplussed and unable to figure out what was going on. An exasperated man leaned out of his car window to explain things to me in slow, clear English. Easy for those who don't have chemo-brain, is all I can say.

Whether you have chemo-brain or not – whether, like me, you have the memory of a fly anyway – this is a golden time for you. Forget names, miss appointments, lose invoices. It all is forgiven when you say, with a catch in your voice but smiling bravely, "I am SO sorry, it must be the chemo, it has this terrible effect on the brain, I can't even remember whether I already told you that I have cancer or not." Chemo-brain can last a while, so you are covered until the time you can replace chemo with Alzheimer's.

Chemo-glow

With a sort of poetic justice, this often accompanies chemo-brain. As your brain shrinks, your looks can improve. Skin tautens, it tans easily and it glows. You may lose a few pounds. It can take ten years off you. On good days, so many people compliment you on how well you are looking that if you had hair you might even be forgiven for thinking it had turned blonde.

Then it strikes you: you are tanned, potentially blonde, you live in an intellectual fog, people wonder if you have had a facelift, you have chic eyebrows (sometimes quite high up your face and surprisingly arched), you have banished chemicals from the kitchen, you drink green juice for breakfast, take 25 vitamin supplements every day, you are dairy-free, gluten-free, sugar-free and red-meat free, you read food labels instead of books, you can nod knowingly when people talk about yoga and mindfulness, you are becoming a bit of a diva, it is all about you and people keep offering you Counselling. *You are turning into a Southern Californian.* Have a wonderful day.

The upside is that I have a renewed respect for my Californian holidaymaker clients, with whom, if I'm being honest, I hadn't always been the most patient when it came to their fanatical adherence to the latest food proscriptions from LA. I tended to get someone else to deal with them.

I once had the PA of a client send me a long list of her boss's dietary requirements and taboos. Along with details of the usual sort of restrictions – medically mandated veganism, gluten sensitivity and lactose intolerance – the instructions on the list had us scouring Greece for weeks trying to source "ancient grains" and investigating the provenance of the glass in which various brands of water were bottled. The PA added in her letter, "But don't be surprised if you occasionally see her nibbling at a piece of chicken." Forewarned is forearmed, so I passed this warning on to the house staff to spare them any such shock. The letter finished with, "Her husband, on the other hand, eats only cheeseburgers and drinks Coca-Cola." And so, between the two of them they licked the platter clean, as the nursery rhyme goes.

Eight months into my sugar-free, dairy-and-red-meat-lite anti-cancer diet, I have overwhelming longings to plunge myself head first into a bathtub full of chocolate cake, brownies, ice cream (which I never even used to like, for heaven's sake), doughnuts and bread and butter with lashings of jam and honey. Only the thought of hungry cancer cells prevents me from doing so – that said, my love affair with green juice, broccoli and kale is never going to turn into a marriage with a diamond jubilee at the end.

The fact that Californians can stick to their horrid and joyless diets without any acute medical need is not to be mocked, and I now take my hat off to their discipline. Perhaps the fear of dying of cancer for them is almost greater than the fear felt by someone who actually has cancer. I do wonder if it is not very unhealthy to live with such fear... I might almost suggest Counselling.

Cancer and the menopause, or the chemopause

This section is not only for female readers. If you are a man who is either married to/living with/working with/raising a female, or you intend to do any or all of the above, you had really better read it as well.

Part of the treatment for most people with breast cancer is chemically inducing (by taking the drug Tamoxifen) the menopause in order to rid your body of oestrogen, which can potentially reactivate your cancer.

This can be brutal, as your body is catapulted – with no warning or gradual progression, and with only an unceremonious yank of the emergency ejector lever – out of its comfortable cruising position and into the outer space of oestrogen deprivation. It objects violently and lets you know in no uncertain terms. However, there is a bright side: we are going to get the menopause anyway, if we are lucky enough to live long enough, and this might just be the smart way to do it. For normal Menopausettes, the truly tiresome symptoms are not something one can whine about, expect any sympathy for, or even display without embarrassment. However, for us Chemopausettes, it is a different matter. Mood swings, irritability, insomnia, aching joints, night sweats, hot flushes and chills – we can put it all down to the chemo and elicit maximum sympathy. Heating up on the Underground when you have failed to get a seat? Pull out your sandalwood fan from your handbag, fan yourself ostentatiously, sigh, then lean down to the closest 20-year-old seated boy (I always choose the 20-year-old boy for the sake of his education, along with the fact that 20-year-old boys shouldn't be sitting anyway, unless they too are have having chemo) and say, "Would you be kind enough to let me sit down? I am having chemotherapy and feeling a bit funny." At least three people will leap up and sweep papers and Burger King boxes off the seats to make way for you. All you have to do is sink down gratefully, flap your fan wanly for a few seconds, then fold your hands in your lap and put on a smile of sweet, patient suffering. Let the waves of support and sympathy wash over you.

Chemopausettes boss it – for a while at least.

However, asking for seats on public transport is surprisingly difficult for some people. One of my radiotherapy nurses, a sweet Irish girl called Mary, is three months pregnant with a sore back. She is on her feet all day long helping others and has a long commute to work. She wears a "Baby on board" badge that London Underground gives out to avoid embarrassing errors. As of yet, no one has paid any attention to it or to Mary. They stare furiously at their mobile phones and hold their newspapers right up to their noses to avoid any eye contact. "Why don't you just ask them to let you sit down?" I asked her recently. "You tell me every day to get up, lie down, move along to the right or left, shift my arm and hold my breath. Just use your nurse voice."

"Oh, I couldn't!" she said, looking distressed at the thought.

"Just try asking them," I said. "People are thrilled to be given the opportunity to do something nice. Don't be so... English." Mary is from County Cork and no one has ever accused her of being too English before. Her patriotic pride stung, she promised to try it. The next day, I asked her how it went.

"Just fine," she said, "it really works. But," and here she hesitated, then said in an abashed sort of way, "I don't think I could do that every day – I would feel too guilty." She really has become too English.

Post-chemo tips

One of the tricky things is, after your cancer treatment is all over, when your hair is back and you look normal, you will still be having hot flushes and aches and pains, won't remember what day it is, will have become addicted to sleeping pills, and worst of all, will know that no one wants to hear a middle-aged lady bang on and on about it. So, how do you deal with that?

The answer is to boldly maintain that, even ten years later, *you are still having chemo symptoms*. You say, "It is sadly a long-term side-effect of chemo that I just have to live with. The symptoms are just like having the menopause." Pause for dramatic effect. "But TWENTY times worse." Then bask in the admiration you get for putting up with what all other women have to put up with in silence. The truth is that they can take hormone replacement therapy and you can't, so it is only fair that you can glean some advantage.

Support for menopause from your medical team is harder to come by – you can't play the cancer card on them, and none of your wonderful doctors want to hear about it. You tell them that acute menopause is much worse than having chemo, much worse in fact than having cancer, but their eyes glaze over, they shuffle papers and say, "Would you like Counselling or a helpful leaflet?" No, you would not like Counselling or a helpful leaflet. You would like OESTROGEN and you would like it now. In fact, you would like to grab your oncologist by the throat and shove your face menacingly into his until he writes you a prescription – that is what other drug addicts do when forced to go cold turkey, but you can't. Failing that, it would be nice if someone were to discover that Nutella is good for all those symptoms. I hope Ferrero SpA is funding clinical research on the matter.

Looking on the bright side, people in my position just have so many cards to play – chemo-brain card, cancer card, chemically induced meno-brain card – one is simply spoilt for choice.

At one appointment, my oncologist was explaining the long-term treatment plan, and the different pills that we could choose from. One made you fat and flatulent, the other was a dynamite oestrogen suppressant, which is the one he proposed. I said, "No, you don't understand. I am already an oestrogen-free zone. I am the black hole of oestrogen, the Bermuda Triangle of oestrogen. If any molecule of it manages to get anywhere near me, I will treasure it for ever. I am begging you in fact to let me have a little oestrogen now and then, just to tide me over..." My rhetoric was having no effect on him at all, so I tried to appeal to his sense of masculine solidarity. "My poor husband," I murmured with downcast eyes, "our sex life, you see, it's, well... you know..."

He was unmoved. "My wife is going through the menopause right now... I'm sure your husband appreciates that after 20 years, there is more to marriage than sex."

We looked at each other glumly and I gave up.

For chemopause tips on the nutritional front, I asked my microbiologist cousin who had sent me the "delicious" bokashi-compost recipe. She sent a learned article from the North American National Institute of Health about the pros and cons of soya as a phyto-oestrogen replacement for cancerous meno-bitches. After wallowing through its pages, the only conclusion I could draw was that unless you are Chinese or a mouse on a high-fat diet, it is not worth the risk. Even if you are Chinese, new evidence suggests that too much tofu can impair the cognitive faculties.

So unless you want to add the tofu-brain card to your hand to complete the Happy Family suit, perhaps it's not worth it – except of course, if you are a mouse on a high-fat diet. In which case, go for it.

It is in fact absolutely scandalous that there is no Menopause Awareness Day* or Matrons Marching for Menopause movement (assuming that with our aching joints and impaired memory we could actually turn up on the right day and march – and ladies, do wear layers that you can take on and off). Nor is there an *I am a Menopauser* ribbon that celebrities of all ages and genders can wear in support. I wish Madonna, Meryl Streep or George Clooney would use their next Grammy or Oscar acceptance speech to stand up for this unloved, mute and unrepresented orphan of a cause that badly needs celebrity parenting. But they wouldn't, because that would take *real* courage, and Hollywood has made the M-word a taboo – if you don't believe in it hard enough, it might disappear.

Unfortunately, the whole phenomenon is still under-researched and untreated, buried in layers of Victorian prudery and overlaid with mockery. Women are woefully unprepared and unsupported for it. Medical profession – wake up! We are a huge market, and we are bad-tempered, sleepless, tearful and spoiling for a fight! Luckily for you, we are also forgetful and have a short attention span, which is probably why you have got away with ignoring us for so long. The time will come, though, when the sisters rise up. Emmeline Pankhurst, where are you when we need you?

Even when the issues are aired, they don't always get taken as seriously as they should. My friend Andrew

---

* Actually, I recently found out, there is one, but not many people are aware of it.

The Meno March

recently called my husband in a state of great excitement. "Florian, now, have you ever heard of *Woman's Hour*?" As my husband is an old-school Bavarian country gent, the question was purely rhetorical. "Well, I have been listening to it all week, as the topic has been the menopause, and guess what! You and I are never going to have sex again."

Manopause

Men don't seem to realise that there is a mano-pause. Only a saint would not feel a secret twinge of *Schadenfreude*. One of the nurses explained that some patients with prostate cancer are put on hormone suppressants after surgery, and they experience the whole menu of mood swings, hot flushes and insomnia. "They moan like mad, poor loves," she said. "Of course, their bitterest complaint is that their wives are totally unsympathetic, and just say, 'Now you know what I went through.'"

The gynaecologist

After persistent whining to my oncologist that he was a man and couldn't possibly understand what I was going through, and that I would rather have cancer again than this meno-nonsense, he referred me to a woman gynaecologist.

Sweating, bad-tempered and aching, I made my way to her rooms the next week only to find that she wasn't there. A timid young receptionist said that my appointment was for the next day. Out came the chemo-tongue. "I distinctly remember that the appointment was for Thursday. This is totally unacceptable."

"Yes, you are right," she said in a professionally calm and soothing voice, "but today is Wednesday..." Abashed, I played the chemo-brain card and slunk off – though it was really meno-brain, which is one of the obstacles one must overcome in order to get an appointment for the treatment of it. A sort of catch-22.

When I finally made it to Dr R's clinic on the right day and at the right time, Dr R turned out to be a tall and glamorous woman with smile-crinkled eyes. I apologised for the mess-up the day before, but she waved her hands around saying: "Oh, I am so glad to hear that. I have clinics on Mondays and Thursdays and, when I am here, I can NEVER remember whether it is a Monday or a Thursday.

You make me feel normal. I do love my job. In fact," and here she looked at me earnestly, "if I had the choice of dying at 56 or 96, I would only give up work if I were going to die at 56."

"Why 56?" I asked curiously. "Why not 59, or 63?"

"Oh, it just feels like the sort of age one could die at if one weren't going to live till 96," she replied.

"Dr R," I said, "we have only just met, but you are as batty as I am."

She looked delighted. "Yes, well we are all bonkers, aren't we? A male student of mine asked me whether he should go for gynie-obst as a career and I told him that the most important thing he should consider is that, if he does, he will for the rest of his life be surrounded by women who are all bonkers: the patients, the nurses, his fellow consultants, the lot of us. He will never see another man again." She paused for effect, then added, "He is thinking about changing to gastro-enterology."

Getting back to business, I complimented her on her receptionist who had handled me so politely the day before, which was a good move as it turned out to be her daughter, covering for the real receptionist who was sick that day.

"I am thrilled she did well," said Dr R, "as I have just had *The Talk* with her."

The Talk, as far as I remember, involves you asking your daughter if she knows how to avoid getting an STD or getting pregnant, while said daughter, aged about 12, rolls her eyes and tells you that your information is totally out of date, and how did you even manage to have three children? I couldn't see how any of that applied to the present situation and looked questioningly at Dr R.

"I have been explaining to her that you have to be very patient and polite with women of a certain age, as we are all menopausal and insane."

Now *that* is *The Talk* that should be on the school syllabus. I noticed at this point that Dr R too was fanning herself, so the rest of the appointment was spent comparing symptoms, and congratulating ourselves for both having turned up at the right time, on the right day, to the right place, and promising to try to do the same in three months' time.

"Would you like an appointment card, an email or a telephone reminder?" asked the real receptionist. "All three please," Dr R and I chorused as one.

I noticed, as I was on my way out clutching my appointment card, that the real receptionist was fanning herself and had a screensaver of a polar snowfield with blocks of ice in the foreground. I think Microsoft has fixed an algorithm that sets polar landscape screensavers automatically for women of a certain age. My laptop has one, my cousin also has one that she can't get rid of. She presses "I don't like this" every day and chooses a sunny beach with palm trees instead, but every day, back it comes. Microsoft knows best.

Once you are admitted to the Secret Sisterhood on the parallel planet of Menopause, you start to recognise the other Sisters and the signs by which they can be identified – a sort of Freemasonry. We don't go in for silly handshakes and weird ritual but we know each other by the vigorous fanning, the continuous taking-off and putting-on again of cardigans, the creaking noise that accompanies our getting up from a chair and the standing in corridors wondering what we were about to do and where we were supposed to be going.

Miraculously, both Dr R and I made it to the next appointment a few months later. She was looking even taller and more glamorous, in a long pleated and ruffled skirt, upon which I complimented her. "Oh! This skirt is *so* not me," she exclaimed, looking pleased, "but it doesn't crease when I sit down and it does swirl so nicely." She pirouetted around the room to show me the full glory of the ruffles. She then sat down again (on her skirt), read her notes about my last visit, knitted her brows and tut-tutted, looked at me intensely and said how much better I seemed. I didn't think I was feeling much better and I asked her why she thought so.

"Well, my notes here say that you were in a terrible state, could hardly walk, hadn't slept for weeks, had lost your memory – so you do seem somewhat bouncier now." She showed me her notes which read like a gothic horror story.

I said that I really didn't think I had been that bad, at which she thought for a minute, then her brow cleared, she smiled beatifically and she said, "Oh, well, perhaps it was me being very hormonal that day – I must look at all my notes from February 4th and see if I gave my other patients such dire reports." I love Dr R.

Personal training and the gym

This is the only time in your life when you will get away with saying you don't want to do press-ups or crunches. "I just *feel* that this is not good for me at the moment, if you know what I mean," you say.

Your trainer, who has been telling you for years to listen

to your body and stop eating chocolate biscuits, will nod solemnly and respectfully and give you a neck rub instead.

Do not make the rookie error of showing this paragraph to the trainer. If you do, when he next suggests that you do some sit-ups and you say with a sad smile, "I am just not feeling it today, my body is saying no," he will reply, cupping his hand behind his ear, "Do you know what? I can hear your body loud and clear saying it wants to do 15 of them – and two sets at least."

Seriously though, even when one is having a "sofa day", movement will make you feel better – I truly think that there is very little that moving around does not improve, whether it's dancing to the radio in the kitchen, walking, sweeping leaves, airing duvets – anything that you can build into your routine will help.

Cancer and TV

You have cancer, so the TV remote control is all yours. No matter what football game is showing, you have priority. Any channel you want: country music, repeats of *Two and a Half Men*, *X Factor*, Welsh sheepdog trials, Welsh anything, in fact, *especially* if it is in Welsh and, if like me, you are neither Welsh nor speak the language. Whatever you want, you get. You know it won't last, so enjoy…

If you are a man, obviously you have always had control of the remote, so there is no new benefit to you.

One awful time, my satellite dish broke and my husband undertook to get it fixed before my next chemo so I could follow the Welsh-language sheepdog trials. "Play the cancer card," I told my husband bossily. He called the repair man and got an appointment to get it fixed in two weeks' time. I was distraught. Perhaps in those two weeks, for the first time ever, Huw Ap Llewellyn *would not get his sheep* and I would miss it.

I rang the repair company the next day and said in a breaking voice how I had cancer and the only thing that made the chemo bearable was watching Welsh-language TV. "Oh," said the lady manager, "why didn't your husband say so? I had cancer five years ago and I know EXACTLY what you mean. Leave it with me."

Twenty-four hours later, my TV was new and improved, with all the buttons now simplified for my chemo-brain – well that was my excuse. I could never make them work anyway.

Always play the cancer card.

One insomniac early morning had me *Keeping Up With the Kardashians*, who decided to fly to Kuba while it was still stuck in the 1950s. I cried with laughter all on my own, as the Kardashians agonised for three days, while being driven around Havana by terrified Cubans, about how to rotate their 25-word vocabulary to allow them to reflect on vitally important matters, such as whether it was passive-aggressive for the shorter, slightly pop-eyed Kardashian to ask Kanye West whether he had liked wearing blue contact lenses.

Back home in LA, Mrs K taught another daughter and a young man who seemed to have been stun-gunned between the eyes (called Scott I think) to cook pasta. Then they all had a family moment discovering that they could have a facial in the steam of the draining colander.

Back in Kuba again, one of the Kardashians summoned up her innermost resources – and ten out of the 25 words at her disposal – to express how life-changing this foreign trip had been: "Toto, I don't think we are in Kanada anymore."

Sheer joy.

The next day, Mrs Kardashian and Kim had one of those therapy-speak fights about some interminably convoluted misdemeanour of Mrs K's involving an Adidas contract, which I have to admit I couldn't quite follow: blah blah, whine whine. Kim was inexorable and won hands down, Mrs K had to apologise. Kim was then stern but forgiving, and they made up. Mrs K looked at Kim nostalgically, and said, "Do you remember when you were little and we made those Kimberley Kupcakes?" Kim nodded, all misty-eyed.

"Yes," said Mrs K, paused, and then she pulled the trigger. "It's not as if you could sing or dance or anything."

I tried to extol the innocent pleasure of the show to my frankly unbelieving sisters, who just looked at each other and said gently, "Khemo-brain."

I was watching one of my favourite Scandi-dramas, the Danish political series called *Borgen* (I don't just watch junk). It had been faultless until series three, episode five, called '*Forensdag Hygge*', or something like that, where the main character – a glamorous ex-prime minister named Birgitte – gets funny pains in her fingers and finally goes to the doctor, the head of department in Copenhagen hospital. We have all been expecting it to be multiple sclerosis, but no, Dr Sorenson orders a mammogram and a biopsy. Oh dear, I thought, I smell trouble. Sure enough, to the accompaniment of ominous music, he tells her she has in fact got "pre-cancerous cells in the upper right quadrant of the right breast", which need immediate treatment. The music swells as she takes this in. Then, just as I feared, Dr Sorenson looks at her and says, "Never underestimate the psychological damage this disease can do to you. At some point you will feel anger and ask, 'Why me?' so please take this number and call my colleague, Professor Sorenson [everyone is called Birgitte or Soren in this series] for Counselling."

"NOOOOO!" I shouted at the screen. "It is just a few pre-cancerous cells. She doesn't need Counselling, she doesn't need shaky hand-held camera effects and eerie music: she just needs to watch some repeats of *Two and a Half Men* and to lighten up. Stop putting stupid ideas in her head!" But of course they couldn't hear me. And, anyway, they only spoke Danish.

I fear the worst. Episodes six, seven and eight, called "*Og Hygge Kounselling*", "*Skipping Kounselling Smorgasbord*" and "*Killing min Kounsellor*", will all have to be fast-forwarded.

It is not that Danes don't have a sense of humour – I remember a short book from my childhood by a certain Piet Hein, called *Grooks* – a collection of small, witty verses, written under the Nazi occupation as a form of resistance, the humour being too subtle for the Nazis' radar to pick up. Sadly, the books are out of print, so possibly beneath modern Denmark's radar too.

So, there we are. Hand-held cameras, eerie music and *Kounselling* it is for poor Birgitte.

Cancer and work

Whatever the doctors threw at me, all I had to do was think that, if it weren't for cancer, I would probably be dealing with a nightmare client or some insoluble emergency that now someone else must deal with. This thought is a very strong relaxant and painkiller.

In fact, cancer gives you the right to avoid all stress – which is highly inflammatory and bad for you – one of those silver linings that is bigger than the actual cloud. This makes you uniquely placed to rearrange your work-life balance. "Yes," you say, "I know, it is a great bore and I am sorry that I can't help and that I am asking you to do this, but you see it would be very bad for my Battle with Cancer." And there ends the argument.

Sadly, I must admit, my little tricks don't always work. Sara, the high-status Rare who is having rather nasty chem-otherapy, happens also to be the brave lady who tries to do our books. It is really rather irritating, as when I can't remember what I asked her to do or how to add up, and then try to play the chemo-brain card on her, she brushes it aside with total recall and perfect clarity, and points out that I am just being sloppy.

To show how bad work can be for the cancer patient, I will just tell one story. Remarkably, I got through the whole of my treatment without feeling sick or throwing up once but, shortly after my final chemo, I could no longer put off an eye-swivellingly boring Skype call with our American software programmer, who is tasked with cleaning up our slightly eccentric invoicing methods. After 20 minutes of interrogation about credit notes and suppliers' receipts and refund notices, a strong wave of nausea swept over me.

"I am so sorry, Patrick, you have done to me what six months of chemo have failed to do: I am going to have to put you on hold while I go and throw up."

When I returned, Patrick, a laid-back midwesterner who drawls a laconic "Gotcha" no matter what jibber-jabber you spout at him, said, "My sister had cancer, don't worry; I understand. She used to throw up whenever she spoke to me too."

Life in the slow lane with a semi-retirement from work has been a revelation to me. For the first time I am seeing how things can manage very well with less interference and a healthy dose of "Do you know what? I think I will just not respond to that email." In fact, if someone says to you, "My friend, you can have a year off work, doing only what you feel like, meeting some wonderful professionals, dropping a few pounds, spending quality time on the sofa in charge of the TV remote control, reading books and having time in the kitchen and the only price to pay now is sore fingernails, temporary loss of hair, some sickness, a few bits of surgery and a month of visiting the radiotherapy suite," well, at the risk of making the lady from Dortmund, whom I quoted at the beginning of the book, even crosser, I would almost say: jump at it.

Cancer and airports

Who knew that travel could be such fun? You order a

wheelchair at the airport (in advance, remember), as you really aren't 100%, even if you can walk perfectly well. You turn up at special assistance and are given a wheelchair and a wheelchair pusher. Curiously, once in your wheelchair, you feel instantly incapable of taking a step more, such is the power of suggestion. You then are whisked away on a VIP track that bypasses all queues. At security, the duty officer kneels next to you, peers lovingly into your eyes and asks if you are in pain. "No," you reply bravely and truthfully, then he murmurs something about asking you if you would allow him to gently feel your turban as a security measure. "Please, go ahead," you reply. You are no longer self-loading freight – you are a precious and fragile VIP. Especially if you have got your best Missoni turban and sunglasses on, and tears are discreetly rolling down your cheeks from underneath.

Your pusher will handle your passport, boarding pass and luggage, will look after you like an angel and will regale you with jokes and stories.

When I was arriving back from Greece to Gatwick airport on a budget airline one evening, the cabin crew made one of their cheery announcements:

"Good evening, ladies and gentlemen, we are pleased to announce that for your safety and convenience, we are about to land at Gatwick South Terminal, instead of North Terminal, as planned, where your family, friends, cars, taxis, etc., are all waiting to meet you *(Sniggering sounds over the intercom)*. If you still wish to go to the North Terminal *(barely stifled laugh)*, there is a convenient, 20-minute walk, followed by a rapid

SELECT

transit that only goes clockwise, so don't get on it in the wrong direction, and then a ten-minute walk to the arrival hall. We wish you a pleasant onward trip and look forward to welcoming you again soon on one of our flights."

This would normally have had me mad as hell and jumping up and down in rage, saying things like, "Are you serious? I am in the travel business and I will make sure that no one will ever fly your airline again, I want to see your supervisor." Meanwhile my family hide in embarrassment and pretend they don't know me. (As I have been cautioned by the police for inciting public unrest in an airport before, their reaction is not unreasonable...)

Not this time, though. I knew that I was a VIP and would be taken care of. Indeed, an asthmatic, his wife, two Plaster Casts and I were tenderly loaded onto an electric cart. As a Cancer Victim, I got to sit next to the driver, while the asthmatic and his wife sat behind, and the two Plaster Casts in wheelchairs were fastened facing backwards at the end. Off we careered, the jokes flying and the driver beeping loudly and carving a path like Boudicca in an armoured chariot through the shuffling herds of pedestrians.

"How are we all doing in the back?" called out the driver cheerfully. "You lost those Plaster Casts a while back," shouted back the asthmatic, and everyone collapsed in gales of laughter.

The driver then took it up a notch. "My best day was when I had to meet the plane from Ibiza and there were three hot blonde girls with broken legs. The first had got rat-arsed in a bar and fallen off her stool, the second had got rat-arsed in a club and fallen off the platform, and the third had got rat-arsed on the beach and just fallen down." We listened fascinated, "Yes," the driver added, a dreamy smile spreading over his face, "that was my best day ever."

The asthmatic, his wife and I felt we were rather letting the side down here but, needless to say, I was delivered immaculately all the way over to the car park in the North Terminal, to the door of my sister's car, where she was waiting for me as planned.

I have a friend called Andrew, a top QC barrister who, following a horrible riding accident, has some difficulty balancing and tends to stagger a bit, so qualifies for a wheel-chair in airports. In addition to the slight stagger, he is very short-sighted and, having a particularly sweet nature, wears a wide and engaging smile on his face as he peers benignly around. Those who don't know him might be forgiven for wondering a little… Customs officers sometimes think he has had too much to drink on the plane, so his devoted and wonderful wife insists that he orders a wheelchair when they travel *en famille*, as it not only avoids that problem, but gives them somewhere to put their hand luggage.

Just recently, he flew back from Ireland with my husband and, as his wife was not with him, he was not needed as a hand-luggage conveyance, so there was no wheelchair. On wending his rather wobbly way through customs on foot, he received a stern look from the immigration officer who noticed he was coming from Ireland, and said in a patron-ising way, "I wouldn't have another drink till you get home if I were you, Sir." Andrew, being the charming soul he is, smiled happily and said, "Oh dear, you are quite right, I won't, thank you!

Andrew as a hand-luggage conveyance

Married bliss

Mrs Patrick Campbell, the Edwardian actress who first played Eliza Doolittle, when asked how she liked being married after turbulent years on the stage, replied, feelingly, "Ah, wedlock, the deep, deep peace of the double bed after the hurly-burly of the chaise-longue." If only.

Finding peace in the double bed when you have cancer is one thing. But when you have the chemopause, the double bed turns into a battleground, I'm afraid. Firstly, the spouse is not allowed to snore; in fact, he is hardly allowed to breathe, certainly not audibly. He is *definitely* not allowed to move around, or get up in the middle of the night, or leave the light on a second after you wish to try to sleep. If he so much as touches you, or comes within six inches of you, he sets off a hot flush or a cold chill, so that is out too. Aching joints and/or post-operative scars mean an elaborate construction of pillows around each part of you, which also heat up and trigger night sweats, so these need to be demolished and rebuilt in a new, cool spot every hour.

Then there is the room temperature. Your head is cold, the left side of your body is hot and sweaty, the right side cold and goose-bumpy. If the spouse so much as tweaks the duvet, everything collapses and you must start all over again. So you develop cunning strategies to retain control – wrapping the duvet round your feet, sticking a toothpick into his side to make him roll over when he snores, or even if he isn't snoring, to be frank, and you just need to vent your insomniac frustration.

You eventually give up, go to the bathroom, and try to cut a sleeping pill in half – to eke out your supply as you are terrified your doctor is going to realise at some point that you have been taking them for six months and he will want to cut you off. You inadvertently crush the pill instead of cutting it, and drop the crumbs all over the floor as your fingers are still chemo-clumsy; you salvage enough from the floor to put in your mouth along with some suspect-looking fluff, and then, if you have managed to get a 20-something-year-old son to move out, you head for his bedroom to try to finish the night off. There you realise that the room smells funky, the lights don't work, and the window doesn't open – but as no one other than the son and his girlfriend has seen this room in daylight for over a year, you didn't know. More things to add to your list of things to do in the morning.

Now that you have become the monster of self-importance, capriciousness and manipulative attention-seeking that you always knew lurked inside, your husband, by contrast, has shown himself to be that paragon of selflessness, sensitivity, strength and kindness that you always told your doubtful parents, sisters and best friends he was. On "sofa days", when you are quite literally toxic, you have tested him to the limit by saying no when he thoughtfully offers to bring you a cup of tea when he is making one for himself, and then, as soon as he has sat down to drink his cup, saying, "Actually, I would like a cup of tea." And then, when he brings it, saying dolefully, "I meant whole-leaf organic white tea with agave syrup," before turning your face to the wall in horror at his lack of consideration.

All this means that you will have to make it up to him in various small ways: for example, encourage business trips abroad and to generally get away more – not because it means you have the bed to yourself, but for his sake. He will love that you are keen for him to visit his family for weekends and stay out late at bridge evenings, it is so thoughtful of you. Ceding control of the TV remote control for a key football match is another useful weapon. Cooking something that tastes nice for once is also good. Don't let him get too used to it: everything in moderation.

A beautiful Greek friend of mine told me that among medical circles in Greece, breast cancer is known as the "divorce disease".

"Oh really," I said with interest. "Is that because famously superficial Greek men can't deal with a prematurely menopausal wife with scars and lop-sided breasts, and so they run off with a 20-year-old bimbo?"

"No, not at all," she explained earnestly, "quite the opposite in fact. Greek mothers have brought up their sons to think they [the sons] are the centre of the universe, so of course they are totally incapable of playing a supportive role to a sick wife. In fact, they tend, when told that the wife has cancer, to turn on her and say, 'What are you doing to me? What have I done to deserve this, how I am supposed to manage?' At which point, the wife runs off with an older, richer man."

She told me of one fun variation on this, which was when a girlfriend of hers was referred to a leading breast surgeon in Greece, who turned out to be an old flame. From then on, whenever she got nicely dressed and put make-up on, her husband would make a jealous scene and say, "I suppose you have a doctor's appointment again with that man who feels your breasts," and insist on going with her.

After all, a man who saves your life and says, "I will not let you die!" is really, in evolutionary terms alone, displaying the ultimate peacock tail. So there is also an option for a breast cancer patient to run off with her doctor. I can just see my poor Mr G's look of horror at the thought.

A good husband is a wonderful source of strength and deserves the final word. At dinner with the children one evening, I asked mine if he thought my two centimetres of newly grown hair would look good if I dyed it platinum blonde. He said yes, he was sure anything would look good.

My eyes grew misty with love and emotion, and I turned to the children and said, "You see, children? That is love – when your wife looks like I do and you still think she is beautiful."

The table fell silent to appreciate the poignancy of the moment; then my husband said, "I didn't say you looked *beautiful*."

Chemo-meno-insomnia

After a while, the joys of *Keeping Up With the Kardashians* and Netflix bingeing do begin to pall, and one would quite like to fall asleep without having to take a pill. Friends recommended that I tried listening to meditation apps, so one night after tossing and turning in bed for hours, even though I am not a meditative person at all, I decided to give it a try.

It took me half an hour to figure out how to download the apps, choose the right ones, and install all the passwords; then, composing myself again, I tried the first one. "Sleep Hypnosis", five stars. A soothing American voice told me to feel my feet, clench them, release them, feel my knees, clench them, release them. She didn't seem to realise that chemo-insomniacs also get cramps at the drop of a hat, so the minute I tried to clench anything, it cramped up and I had to get out of bed and hop around till the cramps went. Eventually we got to "and clench your scalp… and release." How the hell do you clench your scalp? And then to the crux of the hypnosis: "I will count down from ten to one, and then you will be asleep… Ten. You are feeling drowsy." No, I thought, I am not, I am just cramping and irritated... "Seven. You are feeling a tingling in your legs." Wrong again, no tingling at all... "Five. You are feeling heavy and relaxed..." At one, feeling the beginnings of an anxiety attack, I gave up and turned to the app called "Meditation for a Quiet Sleep".

This was another soothing American who started off with "Make an effort to identify the stressful thoughts that are keeping you awake." I didn't have any stressful thoughts other than thinking that these apps were not working, but he was keen that I should identify some, so I spent ten minutes thinking of things that might be stressing me. Then he said, "And now tell yourself that these thoughts are not stressing you." Great. I turned to the last app, which was called "Soothing Sounds to Fall Asleep to".

There were 25 of these to choose from. I played for some time with "gentle rain", "rain storm", "rain on roof", just to hear what the difference was; then I tried "eternity music", but I gradually began to discern where the pattern repeat lay and then it got irritating. I tried "slow waves" but the sound of surf has always made me anxious, as on a Greek island it means that the wind is coming up and you have to rush out and bring in all the cushions. The "waterfall" made me want to go to the loo, and why would "thunder" or "white noise" (a.k.a. radio static) make anyone sleepy? There wasn't a "Soothing American voice telling you to relax", so I looked at my watch, saw it was three in the morning and took two sleeping pills.

Online shopping

This is one of the best therapies I know. The daily delivery of parcels – books, turbans, make-up, food supplements, evening gowns – and the daily returning of parcels by children who are now stepping up, and will cheerfully run down to the post office as often as you need.

The daily delivery is apparently particularly therapeutic for people who were slightly homesick at boarding school, where the arrival of a parcel from home triggered so many neural charges in the pleasure areas that we are apparently still hardwired for this. Like Pavlov's dog, really. Parcel = home = love = mummy and daddy. We get a disproportionate charge of serotonin and its well-known healing effects.

Now, this is important: the therapy lies in *receiving* the parcel, not necessarily in its contents. Always send everything back, except turbans and earrings, as your weight will invariably change once the chemo is over and you are taking Tamoxifen for the next ten years.

I slightly overreached myself ordering a vast rug, which we are now stuck with as unfortunately no one is offering to take it down to the post office for me. So do be careful.

Cancer and social media

I probably wouldn't ever have announced on social media that I had cancer, but I was outed by Lucy on Facebook, who is as inept at clicking the right buttons as I am. I then felt obliged to post an upbeat picture of myself in my most beautiful hat to reassure friends that I was fine, and try to staunch the flood of concern, but primarily as an excellent way to plug the website of my milliner goddaughter who had made the hat (cordeliabradleymillinery.hk). Within seconds it seemed, I had a flood of, "Wow, you are so brave and inspirational" messages – I have a lot of American Facebook friends who are generous with praise. I posted back, "No, I am not, you are missing the point, I am just showing you my fabulous 1920s flapper hat that you can order from Cordelia Bradley!" This generated another flood of "Wow, that is so brave and inspirational" messages, so I gave up.

As a Cancer Victim, every single event thereafter that you post on Facebook gets maximum support, which is lovely, but I had so many messages that I had to write a general "Thank you for being my friend" message, which in turn got so many " No, thank you for being my friend" messages in reply, that I am now faced with having to write "Thank you for thanking me for being your friend", which will also get a flood of replies, and I am wondering how to break the virtuous circle... Facebook, please advise on the etiquette.

Telling one's circle of friends can pose a bit of a quandary – people want to know how you are doing, but hesitate to ask – they don't want to be a bother, they aren't sure how to ask, whether they should ask or how frequently. If they hear nothing, is that good or bad? It is a minefield of very British, hand-wringing, distress-filled awkwardness. I think the best thing, as usual, is to take control, solve the problem and put everyone out of their misery. Linda, my friend with the very earnest oncologist, recently sent this group email, which I thought was both charming and classy:

> Dear All,
> I am sorry to send out a general email, but I can never remember who I've told, or when.
> Also, astonishingly, I get bored of talking about me.
> So, this is just to keep you all up to date, and doesn't necessitate a reply.
> [Then came a brief executive update of her situation.]
> Those of you who know me well may think "She could have called me."
> Others will say "I hardly know the woman, why is she telling me?"
> The answer to both is that it is easier for me, and I've been told to take things easy!
> Love, Linda.

My solution was to start (alright, to get a child to start for me) a WhatsApp group to keep a few far-flung friends and relatives apprised so they didn't need to keep calling my husband to see how I was.

It is crucial to keep your postings to an absolute minimum so as not to burden others with an avalanche of pinging and bleeping. Choose seminal moments when you need extra support, like when you cut your long ponytail off and you want everyone to tell you that you are beautiful, or when you come out of hospital and you would rather like people to send you flowers as it is January and bleak. Only the absolute necessities.

When in mid-treatment, a foolish nephew was reported

on WhatsApp as "Harry has left the group", before I had told everyone that all had gone fine and I was going to be OK, there was a general intake of WhatsApp breath, and that is one nephew who won't be inheriting anything.

Me and Angelina Jolie

As quite a few women in my family have been down this road before me (my own mother had breast cancer which metastasised to her liver when she was 71), it seemed sensible to consider taking a genetic test to see if the BRCA gene, so beautifully highlighted by Angelina Jolie, was one that she and I had in common. It would be quite something to have a genetic resemblance to her, so I went along to a mildly depressed genetic consultant who specialises in taking large sums of money off you at first handshake, since most of his clients decide to take it no further, and the man must live.

One can be tested for dozens of genes which all predict the likelihood of cancer of the something, but as most of those cancers are not screenable, it is almost best not to know and most people don't bother.

I dutifully sent off a swab to California to make sure that all females downstream from me were OK, and was glad to hear that Angelina and I have nothing in common.

Much more exciting is the ancestor genetic test that one can do, which tells you where your early ancestors came from. My mother was 100% middle European Jewish, my father Greek and, like most Greeks, mildly xenophobic and anti-Semitic – Byzantines good, the rest of the world barbarian. There was no discrimination – all barbarians were equally inferior. Peoples of whom he disapproved included the English, the Irish, Scots, Jews, Armenians, Turks, Israelis, Lebanese, Bulgarians, Romanians, Ukrainians, Germans, Americans, Austrians, Dutch, Scandinavians, Swiss, Portuguese, Hungarians, Belgians, Slavs and Arabs. Iranians were left in peace as old neighbours. China and India never really impinged.

Exempt from my thrice-married father's list were pretty or charming women, the French, Italians (who were sort of family), and finally, surprisingly, Canadians. He had lived very happily for some years in Canada, to where he had been sent by his family with wife number two and daughter, to get away from a very awkward situation with an actress back in Athens, who didn't recognise an exit line when cued for it. He loved Canada, marvelled for the rest of his life at the goodness and decency of the Canadians, though he never attempted to emulate them; in fact, he met my mother (wife number three) while he was in Canada, still married to wife number two, and thus had to emigrate again, this time back to Europe, from where he continued to maintain his Canada-worship.

Back to the genetic testing: I sent off a tube of spittle – this time to Seattle – and two months later got the results. I was 56% Jewish. Maths was never my strong point, but my father's xenophobia and mild anti-Semitism was in trouble. Not only was there a stray 6% Jewish component, unaccounted for if only my mother was Jewish, but there was also 2% West Asian, and a smattering of Iberian and North African. Widespread ancestor testing could probably fix a lot of intolerance in the world. I noted that the firm doing the test wisely stipulates a 5% margin of grey area in their findings, to fend off trouble.

Cancer and Chinese calligraphy: "strong but wrong"

Confucius described calligraphy as the trace of a claw on paper left by a bird when it alights for a moment and then flies away again. You should be able to see where the bird came from, how fast it flew, how long it rested, and how it flew off again, all from the trace it left. The brushmark is the trace of your bird, your "chi".

I studied for a few years with Zhao Yizhou, a genius who had done his first piece of calligraphy as a child, when he had been forced to write a long document denouncing his parents for being bourgeois enemies of the state. He displayed the patience of a saint with me. I gave up after a while as I was never going to be any good; I lacked the virtues of refinement and modesty requisite for truly fine calligraphy, and was more of a "splash as much black ink around as energetically as possible and move on to the next character in the hope that things will get better" sort of student. I do think that optimism helps in most things… Yizhou's comment was always "Very strong 'chi', but calligraphy no good."

The idea of calligraphy is to open yourself and your own "chi" or life-force to the cosmic *Chi*, and allow it to guide your brush. Do not impede it with your will or ego. This is why it can be used as a diagnostic in Chinese medicine; if your "chi" is blocked or weak, it will show in your brushwork. Striving for refined and modest calligraphy will reduce your ego, tame your will, heal your blockages, and put you in tune with the cosmos. Sadly, the cosmos and I were not even nodding acquaintances.

Now, with more time on my hands, I rang Yizhou to ask if I could resume lessons, I warned him that it was back to basics as my "chi" is clearly compromised at the moment.

At the beginning of every lesson, my hand shakes, the brush trembles and hovers and is incapable of leaving a straight line. The prized line with "muscle and bone" is beyond me, and my bird is obviously not flying well at all. It is flying like a stricken aeroplane, leaving skid marks, aborted approaches and the odd crash landing... "Very weak," says Yizhou.

But, after an hour of feeling for my "chi", letting it override my own efforts, the lines are straighter, the ink flows, there is bone and muscle in the line, and a delight in the feeling of returning power. "Chi is very strong again, but calligraphy still no good," says Yizhou.

We smile at each other happily, things are back to where they should be. I go away with homework under my arm feeling totally cheerful and invigorated.

Thank-you gifts for surgeons and oncologists can be tricky – a few years ago, my oncologist was given a golden model ship by a grateful VIP, and he has slowly amassed a collection of model boats. "Do you like ships?" I asked one day, hoping for a clue as to what to give him. He paused for a second. "No, actually, not especially, what I really like is a nice bottle of wine."

As for Mr G, my surgeon who is of Chinese origin, I

thought I would give him a personally painted piece of calligraphy, and asked Yizhou what would be appropriate to write. The Chinese are very conservative and formulaic with their messages, so Yizhou's unhesitant answer was, "Much luck and big prosperity".

"I am not sure I want to wish him big prosperity," I said. "His prosperity means lots and lots of surgeries, and if I am unlucky, it might mean that I am the one who will be having those lots of additional surgeries. Let's not tempt fate."

"Ok," said Yizhou, "What about 'Much luck and big happiness'?"

The character for "much" is easy and satisfying to write, so is "big". "Luck" is also lovely to write. But "happiness" is an absolute shocker.

I spent my hour's lesson trying to write "happiness", getting crosser and crosser, banging the brush and ink about angrily without the slightest trace of cosmic harmony.

"What about just writing 'Much big luck'?" I finally suggested. "I am sure he is already happy enough, and big luck is a win-win situation for both him and me." Yizhou looked at the ink-spattered table and the huge pile of scrumpled-up paper under it, and nodded gently, "Perhaps that would be best. You can write it very big so it fills up the paper."

Mr G did in fact look very pleased when I gave it to him, even if he had been expecting a bottle of Lafitte, and said what an unusual present it was. I pointed out in a fit of uncharacteristic honesty that I had by mistake stamped my red-ink signature upside-down, but Mr G said very nicely that the Chinese find upside-down signatures charmingly modest – as if one were not worthy of being the right way up, and particularly auspicious as the character for upside-down is only two strokes more than the character for the Tao or Dao – used in the phrase "good fortune has arrived".

Much big happiness

"Oh," I said, "that is nice; so in fact, you can hang the whole thing upside-down for extra luck!" Mr G's eyebrows moved to resume his usual expression of bafflement at my stupidity, and he said in a puzzled way that that would defeat the purpose as the signature would then be the right way up, so we agreed to leave it the way it was.

Chemo-sight

Despite what your oncologist, your optician and your health insurance say, chemo does affect your eyesight. For the worse, naturally. Your short-sighted eye will become more short-sighted but somehow not save you from needing reading glasses any more, since your long-sighted eye has become much worse, as has your astigmatism. You no longer have any focal point at which you can see anything properly without glasses. Each eye focuses at independent times and lengths from the other, and vitreous membranes fall from your cornea like petals from a cherry tree.

I bought a leather necklace with a ring on the end, from which I could hang several pairs of glasses, all of which fell off and got lost, until I finally also lost the leather necklace. So, what with the tears that also fill my eyes, I really can't see that much at all. It generally doesn't bother me, as the world just looks like a Van Gogh to me, and it means that you only read the really interesting bits of the newspapers – ideally with pictures, like what the Duchess of Cambridge is wearing. The world gets much nicer. And your optician, who is giving you eye tests and making you three pairs of new specs every three months, gives you a discount.

You may find, like me, that your goodwill and energy can get a bit out of hand… I saw a lady approaching in the street with a marvellous hat on. It looked like a fur band with a silken meringue-shaped affair on top and, as I am rather into hats now, I wanted to know where she had got it. As she drew close to me, I beamed at her and started to say, "I just love your h…" but stopped short of saying "hat" as I saw, just in time, that it wasn't a hat at all but a manky, fake-fur headband with her real hair sticking upright from it, badly dyed blonde with roots, quite horrible; no wonder she looked so taken aback. I finished the sentence with "I love your h…eadband", marvelling at my own great presence of mind.

Small treats

- Sniffing shampoo – brings it all back, metaphorically speaking of course.
- Turbans – I have a collection of around 25, most of which I continue wearing now I have hair again – how could I have missed out on a whole body part to dress and decorate all these years? I am making up for lost time. Missoni are the clear leaders.
- All those big, 1980s single earrings you have kept in the vain hope their mate will turn up? Clip a big sparkly one onto the top of a leopard-print turban and feel like a maharajah's pet cheetah.
- Little Ondine nail polish – this is non-toxic, dries instantly, covers your nails for when they get sore and discoloured (one of those small indignities of chemo) and it peels off easily. As your nails also peel off easily, this is a really good tip.
- Wunderbrow – terrible name, but a brilliant way to quickly paint on lovely eyebrows even with a wobbly hand and blurry vision.
- Sunglasses – you are medically mandated to wear large sunglasses even on a grey winter's day.

- Rain and drizzle – do your worst, I am frizz-free and immaculate in my turban.
- Wondering whether to make the leap from dyed hair to grey? You have a unique opportunity to make a fresh start and go grey without having to camouflage dyed ends and grey roots. *If you want.* In my view, going officially grey after years of dying your hair must be a bit like coming out in a slightly homophobic society – you admire the ones who do it, but have no intention of following their example.
- Watching for your hair to regrow – like waiting for the first daffodils of spring. Sadly, the hair that grows back first and fiercest is the hair on your legs; while the fuzz on your head is warm and soft and like having an ostrich chick perched on your head for you to stroke whenever you want. Other people will also want to stroke your head, which is rather nice.
- The day when you can wash your new hair – it doesn't need washing as it is only 5cm long, but oh, the bliss!
- Burping – if you have married into and created a Germanic family, you will know all about the honourable hobby of seeing who can burp the loudest. You now have a sporting chance of beating them all.
- Foraging with the dogs for wild herbs for juicing – the dogs think you have finally come to your senses and realised that hunting for mice is what you like doing. Their enthusiasm is only slightly marred for you by the fact that they tend to dig where you are trying to forage.
- Hot flush on command – you may not be able to prevent them, but you can learn to summon one up when needed. Too cold to get out of bed on a winter's

morning? Roll around vigorously three times, draw the sheet over your head, and boom! After 30 seconds you will be steaming hot, you can fling the duvet off, and jump happily into a healthy, cold shower.

Things not to say to a cancer patient:

"Did you catch it early?"
If the answer is "yes" that's fine, but the answer may be "no", which could be a bit of a conversation stopper unless you are close to the cancer patient.

"My aunt/sister/mother had the same thing and is fine."
You mean well, but your relatives' experience, in all likelihood, has nothing to do with your cancer patient's experience. Talk about your aunt/mother/sister, but don't draw any conclusions from that.

"Did I just see you eating chocolate biscuits??"
There is no point scolding, what you should do is eat the chocolate biscuits yourself to remove the temptation from the cancer patient.

"Now that it is all over and you are well again, could you please…"
This is generally followed by requests to do all the boring chores that you have been doing for the cancer patient, and can't wait to hand back to him or her to do.

"That was not ten push-ups, I was counting, it was five."
Yeah yeah…

"Do you mind if I go skiing for a week?"
Well, what is the cancer patient supposed to say to that without sounding like a real bitch? What she will have to say is "Of course not, darling, have a lovely time." *As you well know.*

"Is cancer contagious?"
This was a real question put to my friend Lucy one day at chemo by someone who was accompanying her. It made the hand of the nurse who was about to insert the chemo needle into Lucy's port shake so much with laughter that she missed her target and stabbed Lucy in the chest. (The answer is, of course, no, cancer is not contagious.)

"I always thought you were too old to have such long hair anyway."
Really not a good thing to say, even if it is true.

"Good afternoon, Sir, what can I get you to drink?"
Said to me by a male waiter with an enviably long and glossy ponytail, when, proudly sporting one inch of new hair, I ventured out for the first time without a turban. I nearly cried, but instead, told him I had cancer and I would accept a complimentary coffee for having my feelings hurt.

"What is for dinner?"
How should the cancer patient know?

"Do you mind if I turn on the football?"
Well of course they do, don't make them say it…

"How does your husband put up with you?"
The answer is obvious: he is a saint.

Things you can say to someone with cancer:

(If you are a husband or partner) *"Can I bring you a cup of tea in bed?"*

"Can I come and see you? I will only stay for an hour…" –
The only-stay-an-hour bit is important.

"May I come and sit with you while you have chemo or take you to radiotherapy?"

"Here is the telephone number of my acupuncturist/nutritionist/faith-healer/other."

"Would you like a neck rub?"

"Would you like to come and stay with us in the Bahamas when it is all over?"

"Gosh you are an inspiration!"

"You have such a beautiful shaped head, you can get away with being bald."

"I have brought you the latest Missoni turban as a present, and some earrings to go with it."

"Dinner is ready!"

"You can call me up for a moan whenever you feel like it, I promise I will not think you are falling apart in general, and will understand that you are just feeling cranky or blue <u>today</u>."

"Don't forget that the new series of The Big Bang Theory *starts today on E4."*

"You will ALWAYS be a trophy wife even if you have developed a bad retail therapy habit, lop-sided breasts, are off-work and are sporting a USA Marines hairstyle."

Surgery

I tried to persuade Mr G, my surgeon, to do a job lot on me when we discussed what surgery he would be likely to perform. I pressed him to remove other bits like ovaries and appendices, on the principle that I don't need them so we might as well take those out too before they get cancerous. He was not keen and I pressed him perhaps a little too much, as he suddenly leaned forward and said, "Let me explain something to you…"

He then went into the gory details about how you are tilted upwards on the operating table when you have a breast lump removed, and if you have your ovaries taken out, you are tilted down, and for appendices you are tipped sideways, so you would end up being spun up and down and around like the contents of a tumble-drier; and if I want that sort of thing I would have to find another surgeon.

I didn't dare ask him about the cataract removal after that, though I thought I might still make a last-minute attempt to get those done when the time came. Perhaps one doesn't need tilting at all for that? I didn't in the end, as the last thing one needs on the day is an angry surgeon. Angry Surgeons sounds a little like a game on a mobile phone, but would be less fun and you would probably lose.

Anaesthetists

My friend Lucy, on her way to her umpteenth surgery texted me:

> Secretly looking forward to the general anaesthetic – those first few seconds – sheer bliss. I hope I have an amenable anaesthetist who will administer it v v slooooooooowly and draw out that woozy feeling. Last time I asked for it v slow they were not amused at all. I tried to explain that if you have to have general anaesthetics all the time then you might as well make the most of them and enjoy them. I think it's my 20th time…

Way to go Lucy. She later posted a photo of herself smiling happily over her post-operation breakfast tray, which was bearing a large mound of scrambled eggs, six pieces of toast, half a pound of bacon, six sausages and a large pot of coffee. So I am guessing she enjoyed her anaesthetic.

Generally speaking, an anaesthetist tries to make you chat while he administers the drug, so he can see when you fall asleep. The usual gambit is "So, what is your line of work?" and then if you answer something like "I work for the Brent Council animal welfare department," he pushes the plunger in quickly.

When you say you arrange villa holidays in Greece, most anaesthetists will pause while they tell you all about their last Greek holiday, their next holiday plans, and ask you to go over the relative merits of the 35 different islands in great detail, so that blessed oblivion can't come soon enough.

This time when I answered the usual "What is your line of work?" by saying that I arranged luxury villa holidays in Greece, my anaesthetist put the syringe down and said, "Gosh, does that exist? Do they get together in a group and book after their operations?" Now, I was the one supposed to be babbling nonsense by this stage, not him, so this was a little worrying. I stared at him in concern. He stared back at me. "Filler holidays," he repeated, "Bottom-lifts, bosom lifts, face-lifts, etc. They go on holiday post-op till the bruises from all the fillers fade, I imagine?"

"Brilliant," I thought as I drifted off to sleep. "Luxury Filler Vacations. A whole new market to open up once I am better."

In fact, the owner of a very pretty house we rent out is a top plastic surgeon, and the reason he rents his house out in summer is that August is high season for facelifts; the chic ladies (and some men) have their faces done then, so they can lie low for three weeks till the bandages come off, then, when their friends all exclaim how well they look, they can wave the compliment away and murmur that they have been in Marbella. The poor chap can't ever take a holiday in August. So there is indeed a market for Five Star Fillers.

In hospital

After my surgery to remove my lump and all my lymph nodes, the nurse looking after me made the assertion, probably correctly, that now was her only chance to make me listen to her advice as I was currently docile and vulnerable, having just come round from the anaesthetic.

"Tomorrow you won't listen to a word I say," she said cheerfully. She then described all the apocalyptic things, like lymphoedema, that would happen to me if I failed to wear gardening gloves or a thimble for the rest of my life, or got scratched by a cat – rather like Sleeping Beauty, if you get pricked on the finger it can lead to terribly inconvenient results. And, really, don't hold out for Prince Charming's kiss, when you only have a little fine fuzz on your head and your digestive system is still a trifle wonky post-chemo. Best to have a Plan B somewhere up your sleeve – along with your lymphoedemic arm.

I like to think the nurses have a "Guide to Patient Stereotypes" to refer to when they size you up. Along the lines of:

Type: Apple-cheeked youngest child. *Action*: Steer clear and don't answer bell.

Type: In total denial, says there is nothing wrong and they'll be going home that evening. *Action*: Give them all the horror stories as soon as they open their eyes.

Type: Weepy and accompanied by 12 close family members. *Action*: Give them the menu and encourage them to order lots of food.

My 27-year-old son had his tonsils taken out a few weeks before my surgery. He had not been to hospital since he was born. His long-suffering girlfriend took him in on the day, stayed with him, and then wrote to me from his bedside: "Well, he knew what to do with the hospital gown, and put it on the right way, but he thought the paper under-wear they provide was a hat and put it on his head. I asked him what he reckoned the three holes were for. He said he thought it was for ponytails. You must be very proud…" She sent a photo as well.

According to my nurse, 20% of patients put these paper knickers on their head.

An addendum to the handbook:

Type: Puts the hospital paper knickers on their head. *Action*: Needs looking in on frequently, and courtesy calls every day for a week after discharge.

My nurse, Sally, was a very chatty and cheerful veteran who had missed her calling as an entertainer. She told me about the spanking new wing of the clinic where Mr G usually operates, but was closed over the holidays. If my surgery had been only a few days later I could have been there, rather than where I was, in the shabby old wing.

"Oh, you wouldn't like it," she said when I asked what it was like. "Cutting-edge modern; the bedrooms are far too big and designer-y, the bathrooms are vast and marble with underfloor heating; everything is electric and push-button; doesn't look like a hospital at all – lights embedded in the ceiling like stars. In fact," she leaned towards me conspiratorially, and whispered, "when a patient wakes up after surgery the first thing they see is the starry ceiling, and we nurses often worry that they think they have died and gone to heaven. What with the echoing marble halls and the harp muzak that accompanies you as you ascend gently to the eighth floor, and everyone dressed in pale blue or white…" her voice trailed off.

She then pulled at a tube that I had been sitting on by mistake that turned out to be the oxygen tube that you put in your nose. "Ha, as students, we used to go and have a quick sniff if we had a hangover after a party, so feel free to use it as much as you want."

I hoped she hadn't noticed that, while I hadn't put the paper knickers on my head, I hadn't put them anywhere else either, so the plastic oxygen nozzle was certainly not going to go up my nose. Who knows who else had sat on it by mistake.

Luckily, she had moved on to her student days so hadn't noticed. "I trained with a real old dragon," she said, while taking my blood pressure. "The matron didn't allow fathers to attend births. She said they cluttered up the place and tended to faint at the wrong time. If they insisted on being there, and did faint, we were instructed to just step over them and leave them where they were. Littered the place, they did."

At the birth of our first child, my husband fainted before anything had even happened, and all the nurses left me on the trolley with a needle in my arm while they fussed around him, so my sympathies were entirely with the matron.

As Sally took my temperature, and saw me peering at the result, she remarked that she had noticed distinct behavioural differences between the patients she had looked after depending on their nationality. In the travel world, we also notice strong behavioural differences, so I asked her to explain, in case they were similar.

"The French are obsessed with their livers. Whatever is wrong with them, they say it is caused by stress of the liver. You tell them that it is because they have been smoking/not exercising/have just given birth/had open-heart surgery, but *non*, it is their liver."

I can vouch for that – as a young art student, I lodged with an elegant but impecunious *comtesse* in Paris, who had nine children and, whenever one moved out, she would take in a lodger. She was tall and thin and dark, looked like Olive Oyl from *Popeye*, and was, I now realise, a saint. She spent all day long cleaning, cooking and rushing around the apartment after children, lodgers and her large and sleepy husband, scaring off any male visitors who dared present themselves. Her hair was always escaping from her swept-up chignon and shedding hairpins. With dust cloths wrapped around her shoes she also polished the floor as she rushed around.

She found me one day boiling an egg for breakfast, and nearly had a heart attack – "*Ma pauvre fille,*" she cried, "An *egg*???? No wonder the English have such bad livers, *quelle idée!*" and then gave her waiting children their richly buttered baguettes to dunk in their huge bowls of milky coffee, and went out on to the balcony for a cigarette.

Sally continued: "The Greeks and Italians, on the other hand, only care about their temperature. They could be haemorrhaging all over the bed, but as long as they haven't got a temperature, they couldn't care less." As a Greek, I can also vouch for that. I happen to know my base temperature is a chilly 35.6, so, as I told Sally, when a doctor takes my temperature and says, "Ah, only 37 degrees, there is nothing wrong with you," I go ballistic, as this is practically delirium territory for me.

"Yes, well," Sally said. "There we are, I could have told you that."

"Go on," I prompted her. "What about the Brits?"

"Bowel movements," she said brightly. "Obsessed. That is why we have All-Bran and stewed prunes and prune juice on the breakfast menu. They could talk about bowel movements all day long. And do."

"And the Germans?" I asked.

"Ah, that is a strange one. They are keen on bowel movements too, but what really matters to them are their feet." This rather nonplussed me, as I couldn't imagine how concern about feet could manifest itself. "Ach, nurse, pleez, can you see if mein feet are still zere?"

I forgot to ask about Arabs, Chinese and Americans, though a Canadian doctor told me that in Canada they say that if a hospital patient is complaining about the food and saying they want to get outta there real quick, they are probably Americans regretting their cheap healthcare trip across the border.

Post-surgery

It is really hard to find the fun in this: things hurt, seize up, and if you get something called a seroma, it is like having a hot, swollen, fluid-filled, angry toad clamped to your ribcage and chewing your armpit with very sharp teeth, and all your surgeon can say is, "You should wear your bra." Oh, yes, right, thank you very much, very helpful. You try wearing a bra that cuts into a hot, swollen, fluid-filled, angry toad chewing your armpit. Honestly.

My advice is much more helpful: whinge, whinge like mad and make everyone else's life as miserable as yours is until it all settles down, particularly if you have been good up till now and they have all had it far too easy and taken you for granted. Mix it up a bit so they don't get bored and they might even start offering to bring you cups of tea in bed. Apparently, some husbands do this even if you don't have cancer or aren't post-surgery with a hot, angry toad clamped on your ribcage.

Your surgeon may well change his tune now that you have been operated on. Pre-surgery, his upbeat view was, "The breast I will operate on will be smaller, firmer and higher, and then, if you want, we can make the other side match so you will have had in effect, a top-notch breast lift."

Post-surgery, he examines his handiwork with satisfaction and then says, "That looks great, and once the swelling

My toad and I want tea in bed please

goes down, gravity will have its way, it will droop and deflate just like the other side, and will be a perfect match, so I don't see any need for further cosmetic work."

Promises, promises, promises.

Radiotherapy

This is the easiest bit, according to many. The only bore for most is the daily trek into the clinic. For me, as a lucky holder of a very thorough private German medical insurance, the daily trek is a constant source of cheer. I love my walk to Harley Street. In fact, I love Harley Street. No tourists shuffling along vacantly, blocking the way, looking for a

Starbucks/safe road crossing/lost child/entrance to Madame Tussauds/somewhere to charge their mobiles. Refreshingly, everyone there is there for some worthy or serious reason; they are delivering blood, they are world-class medics, they have an interesting disease, they are coping with immense issues, they are part of a highly skilled team. It is the most purposeful street in London. It is also by now like a club for me. I can buzz my way through any number of front doors, nod to the receptionist, use the loo, have a complimentary cup of coffee and a rest. No one is the slightest bit bothered and it feels like an awful lot of them have seen my breasts anyway.

The only downside is that you have to run the gauntlet of the nicest shops in London, selling everything from scented candles and design books to sunglasses, fresh fish, clothes and chocolates. As I feel after every treatment that I deserve a little reward, the gauntlet-run often ends in failure, but I am unusually chic as a result. I don't even regret the ruinously expensive rain cape that I bought; although my children greeted it with howls of "Oh my God, you must think you are a Hobbit or something." I am sure it will come in very useful. After all, I will be on pills for the rest of my life that make you fat and flatulent, so a cape is going to be a brilliantly useful long-term investment.

Preparation
The first appointment for radiotherapy is to go over all the side-effects, plot the angles of X-rays and formalise the position in which you lie on the machine so it can be replicated every day.

My radiotherapist is an elegant lady with a streaming

cold. When I arrived for my first appointment, she must have had some free time before my arrival, as on her very smart flat-screen computer embedded into the surface of her desk, I could see her guiltily left-swiping lots of very familiar websites – Net-a-Porter, Finery London, Matches. She was looking for a winter coat, which, by late January and the sound of her sneezing and coughing, was rather shutting the stable door after the horse has bolted.

"We have to look at screens so much while talking to patients, that we thought it would be nice to have the screens embedded in the desk so we aren't hidden behind a computer," she explained apologetically.

She started off by drawing a diagram of my breasts as seen by someone standing at my feet were I lying on a table – it reminded me irresistibly of one of those Old Master paintings of cadavers by someone Dutch, called "The Anatomy Lesson" or "The Doctors". She drew two large and upright mounds, with a heart and a lung underneath. "I hope you aren't an artist," she added.

"I am actually, but no pressure," I answered, just for fun.

"Oh," she said, then rubbed out the firm, upright mounds, took a closer look at me, and said, "Well, let's just flatten these out a bit and slide them round to the sides; there, that is better. Now we can see where the line of the X-rays will fall." No one wants me to have a firm high bosom.

The official, pre-therapy talk about the side-effects of radiotherapy is always the worst part. Imagine a risk assessment team scrutinising your morning routine:

"Getting out of bed can sometimes lead to falling onto the floor and a broken leg, or, if the head strikes the corner of the bedside table, death."

"Showering is to be undertaken only with due care and only if you have not already broken your leg getting out of bed, as wet surfaces may be dangerous and cause you to slip. Have a towel and a panic button within reach at all times."

"Brushing your teeth should be part of your daily routine. Should you apply too much pressure, this may result in receding gums and bleeding, which can also lead to unsightly exposure of tooth root. Some people prefer to have all their teeth removed in preventative surgery. We have a useful leaflet to inform you about prosthetic teeth, the problems associated with mastication and a list of professionals to offer you Counselling. If you find this leaflet helpful you can donate to our charity, Gums R Fun, on the form in the inside cover."

"Shoes that do not fit perfectly may cause lesions to the skin on the toes or heel, or both, which can, if untreated, become infected, and in some people turn into necrotising bacterial infection. If you are unsure as to whether your shoes fit perfectly, avoid walking long distances in them, or wear slippers. We run a weekly course which many people find very valuable, with a follow-up workshop called 'Heal and Soul', where refreshments and entertainment are provided by the 'Blista Sistas'."

"Boiling water for coffee is not recommended as scalding could occur, and you may experience painful burns to the tongue and mouth which can result in temporary or permanent loss of sensation (NB people who have already hit their head on the corner of a bedside table are a higher risk group)."

ILEANA VON HIRSCH

"If you repeatedly experience these side-effects do NOT attempt to get up in the morning and get dressed unless under medical supervision."

On the bright side, when you turn out to be one of the lucky people who don't break their legs getting out of bed or drop the kettle full of boiling water on their slippered feet, you do feel rather smug.

Then come the consent forms. "Do you give consent for us to take a photograph of your arms in the position that they are in now, so we can replicate it? Do you give consent for us to take a photo of your face so we can make sure we have the right person on the scanning bed every day? These pictures will not be posted on social media or published anywhere." Well, yes, of course you give consent. You also wonder who would not give consent, possibly those who have trouble breathing or can only boil water under medical supervision.

When it was all over, the nurses said goodbye to me and hoped it wasn't too bad.

"No, not at all," I said, "I have a meeting with my accountants now, so this was the high point of my day."

"Golly," they said, looking pleased, "No one has ever said that to us before."

How to breathe
The nurse, having gone over in solemn detail all the things that could happen now or 20 years hence, will then tell you that the most important thing is to relax on the scanning bed, or it will all go wrong on the day. On top of all these

doomsday scenarios, the machines blow a stiff, arctic breeze over you, as they are kept at a low temperature to avoid them overheating. Relaxing is harder than it sounds when you are shivering with cold.

The nurse starts in earnest: "As we explained in all the pre-scan talks, you unfortunately have a complicated scan, and so you have to take a deep breath when we X-ray, and hold it for ten seconds. You may find this distressing and difficult, and some people can suffer from hyperventilation or panic attacks. To help you, here is a pair of goggles that contain a visualisation of your breathing so you can see how deep you need to breathe and how to count to ten. Shall we have a couple of practices first? Just take a few minutes to compose yourself and let me know when you are ready."

Feeling increasingly nervous, as you had not realised that breathing was so distressing or difficult, you take a couple of minutes to compose yourself, while getting colder and colder and, preparing to hyperventilate, you get ready to take a deep breath.

You breathe a couple of times, counting to ten, and the nurse squeals in happy excitement, "Oh, that is brilliant, you are so clever, you got it right first time; you breathed perfectly, *and* held it for ten seconds. That is wonderful. We don't really need to practise any more if you feel you can breathe like that on the day."

I promised I could repeat that amazing feat whenever they wanted. You do have to slightly wonder about the people who need to practise... total morons, one might say.

Should you have low self-esteem issues, being

congratulated on knowing how to lie still, count to ten and take a deep breath at the same time is very gratifying. Radiotherapy didn't seem like it was going to be too bad.

Hubris

Definition: In Greek tragedy, excessive pride towards or defiance of the gods, leading to nemesis [and possibly Counselling…]

So it turned out that, after all, I couldn't take a deep breath and count to ten. At least not in a consistent way that I could replicate every time. The thin green line of your breath on the visualisation goggles you're given to help you see how far to inflate your lungs must first hit and then rest squarely within the narrow band of blue. If at any point while you are counting to ten, your thin, green breath line wavers even a fraction of a millimetre outside the blue band, this will cause the machines to stop in their tracks and then you must start again.

Day one of radiotherapy was OK, day two was hit and miss, on day three, despite practising at home to the amusement of my family, I still couldn't do it and was getting worse, not better. The rage and frustration growing inside me that I couldn't manage this simple thing, and therefore ranked along with the despised morons, made my chest heave even more with uncontrolled breathing. On day four, when the first breath I took shot way up above the blue band and showed no signs of coming down again, I burst into tears and wept heartbrokenly on the scanner. The machines all waved their arms around in horror, beeped in alarm and crashed to a halt. The room filled with people, a minder bustled me off into a little room, and before I knew it, a nurse with Team Leader on her badge, was giving me Counselling.

"Is it the idea that you have cancer?" she asked kindly.

"No," I wept.

"Is it the surgery or the chemo?"

"No," I wept.

"Are you feeling lonely and isolated with no one you can really talk to? Are you asking 'why me'?"

"No," I sobbed.

"Are you questioning your mortality and the meaning of life? Perhaps you have been in denial and are now having to face all the issues of your 'journey' that you have been suppressing, and haven't been able to talk to anyone, have always had to put on a brave face, but you need to be allowed to be weak and frightened – is that it?"

"NO!!!" I wept, "None of the above, that is all fine. I am crying because *I can't hit the frigging green line* and you must all be sitting there watching the monitor thinking 'Silly cow, why can't she breathe and count to ten so we can all go home?'"

"Don't worry," she said, with the suspicion of a smile on her face, "no one is sitting here thinking that you are a silly cow – you can take as long as you like over this, some people never manage it at all and we have to do it another way. In fact, we see this all the time. People like you who are..." – and here she stopped to find the right words to describe people like me in a diplomatic way, and then gave up. "*People like you* usually break down on day three or four of radiotherapy. You have done what everyone says is the hard part, this is supposed to be easy, and suddenly, you can't control something. Don't worry, you don't have to be perfect, and if you can't hit the green line every time we will do it another way. Have a good cry and it will all be better." She added anxiously, "I can't give you a tissue, as we are taught that offering a tissue is a signal that you want the person to stop crying and, with *people like you*, it is very important to cry now and then."

Still slightly wondering about the "people like you" bit, I stopped crying, and as there were no tissues on offer, wiped my eyes and blew my nose into my hospital gown. After a cup of tea, we managed to finish the session. One tip I can pass on – if you wear thick ski-gloves or mittens, they cushion your hands resting in the brackets and keep you warm. You may feel a bit kinky lying on a bed in your undies and a pair of strangler gloves, but trust me, it is a huge help.

On a more serious note, I learned that things will take their course; whether I can do the breathing perfectly every time, or never get the hang of it, really is of no interest to the universe, which will go on expanding into emptiness. Thank you to nurses Zeinab, for gently pointing this out to me, and Niamh, for giving me half her Kit-Kat. Sorry about the hospital gown.

Needless to say, the following day I performed impeccably, every breath a success. "It doesn't get better than that," they beamed at me, but I am now a wiser and humbler person, and I know that if I don't perform perfectly each time, it couldn't matter less.

The day the stressful breathing-radiotherapy ended was probably the best day of my whole treatment. This is the only time when you are asked to perform – a hushed silence and red light blink as the stage empties, a camera and bank of monitors looking down at you; take one, take two... All that is missing is the clapper-board. Stage fright is the best way I can describe it. I don't expect to miss anything about that bit at all.

The waiting room

In the radiotherapy waiting room, regulars smile politely every day to each other and dive straight into a slightly out-of-date real estate or fashion magazine. You can tell the regulars by the fact that they know how to use the incredibly complicated coffee machine which is almost as sophisticated as the radiotherapy machines and seems to have even more finely calibrated functions. In general, it takes patients three days to work out how to get the drink of their choice. On the first two days you have to ask the kind receptionist to do it for you.

The other day, a well-dressed and imposing woman was sitting there – in my seat actually – clearly a new girl, in spite of having successfully operated the coffee machine, talking quietly and firmly on the phone while rustling a sheaf of medical papers.

"Please make sure that the outer tube is calibrated to 5.5 mills... Yes, only use the blue tape, not the green tape. Mr B says this is very important. The small tube should have a diameter of 2.4 mills, the lock should be off... and make sure that all surfaces are very clean and dry before applying. I have looked at the diagrams and the different perspectives all seem to align perfectly, so we can go ahead."

I was hugely impressed at how knowledgeable this

woman was about her treatment and how detailed her understanding was about the whole scanning and X-raying process. Perhaps she was a doctor herself. Imagine how nerve-wracking it must be to be a doctor yet have other people treat you. Like being a pilot and flying economy. I felt that perhaps I had been a bit sloppy myself, as I had no idea what diameter any of the tubes were, and it had not occurred to me to ask to see any diagrams.

"Fine," she continued, checking things off her list. "Well then, my daughter will let you in, the electrician is already there, and when you have finished in the small bathroom, you can start in the downstairs loo."

I still think she might have been a doctor, and felt rather sorry for her plumber, though distinctly better about my lack of interest in the alignment of my scans with the arc of the X-rays.

Some curious side-effects

One unexpected consequence of all the high-tech treatments that I have had is that I am now very careful about crossing roads – I feel a huge responsibility, in view of all the time, effort, money, skill and technology that has gone into keeping me healthy, not to come to a sticky end stepping out in front of a bus because I was on the phone or couldn't be bothered to wait for the traffic light to change. I can just imagine Mr G, Professor E and the whole team's reaction if that happened... "Silly Cow" doesn't begin to describe it.

For the five weeks of radio treatments, you whip off your

top every day in front of a mix of familiar faces and total strangers as you are pushed and prodded by new nursing staff: "Hello, I am Jane, we haven't met yet,"/"Hello, I am Derek, we haven't met yet". (Either there is a remarkably high turnover of radiotherapy nurses, or else no one wants to have me more than once a week...) Anyway, I got so used to wandering around chatting half-naked in front of strangers, that I often had to be reminded to put my clothes back on before heading home. This has the very awkward side-effect that, even now, whenever I turn up for any kind of appointment anywhere, my instinct is to say hello, shake hands, and then take off all my clothes.

Faith, hope and innumeracy

At some point, you are faced with updated statistics on re-occurrence of your cancer, survival, etc., etc. Now, I have no feel for numbers, I can't be trusted with zeros or decimal points, and am resigned to having a blind spot as far as anything quantifiable is concerned. At university, I read philosophy, politics and economics (one had to do all three for at least one year), and the economics part was always a disaster. My tutor was a dry, dusty woman called Theo, who couldn't quite understand why I had been admitted in the first place and I can't say she was wrong. At the end of first year, as I was standing in the queue waiting to enter the exam room behind a friend of mine who was very good at numbers, I just had time to hiss, "Can you remind me what interest rate means?" She looked at me in disbelief, searched for the right words to suit my level of understanding, and came out with, "Imagine a Red Indian gives another Red Indian an ear of corn to plant. When the harvest is over, the one who borrowed the corn gives his friend back the ear of corn, but also a few extra grains to plant as a thank you. Those grains are the interest." We said Red Indians in those days.

I managed to write two essays about Red Indians planting corn, and then, by dint of copying her graph (she sat in front of me and my eyesight was quite good in those days), I squeezed a third question out – although, as I couldn't quite read how she had labelled her graph parameters, I think I wrote Red Indians on one side of the grid, and Ears of Corn on the other. Anyway, it ended well as I was able to drop economics after that.

My point is that having no feel for numbers is a good thing when it comes to medical statistics. I can see that if you have a 95% chance of living happily ever after, it is nice to know, but in real life statistics are abstract things that refer to a vague concept called "other people".

"Other people" are the ones who win the lottery, marry George Clooney, invent Tetra Pak, become Hollywood's highest paid actor, start a tech empire from their bedroom aged 24, have flawless skin and naturally straight and shiny hair. I have never been one of the "other people". So now, when "other people" are the ones who don't survive their cancer or get hit by a bus, it is of no relevance to me what-soever; I just carry on doing my best to make sure I am never "other people": eating healthily, laughing frequently, ignoring anything inconvenient, hoping for the best, having faith and trusting in my innumeracy.

Convalescence

If you, like me, have never been to the Maldives or had a Caribbean holiday, this is clearly the place to start. Being in the travel world myself, I can spot a time-waster a mile away, and have put up with so many that I now feel no guilt at all in leaping over the other side of the fence, and becoming a time-waster myself with an unfortunate travel agent for the Maldives.

We discuss each atoll, the spas in the various resorts, the outdoor rain-water showers, the dhow trips, the over-water villas where you sit with your legs dangling over your deck, toes touching the lagoon below, and watch Nemo and his friends swimming beneath. Bicycle hire, paddle-board hire, wheelchair at the airport naturally... Which resort has the whitest sand, the bluest water, the quietest guests, and which has the best massages under the palm trees.

Having exhausted one particular travel pro, you can move on to Anguilla or St Lucia, Mauritius or the Seychelles. You know you are never going to make it to any of them once you hear the price.

The travel agent can be mollified with any number of great reasons why you can't commit: you don't know when the treatments will end, when you will be cleared for travel and if indeed you can be exposed to strong sun.

But the pleasure of looking at these beautiful places, imagining yourself there, getting the upgrades, the honeymoon suites, and then, and this is the key bit, *not having to go*, make it the best kind of convalescence. A virtual convalescence trip.

It reminds me of the old joke my Hungarian relatives

used to tell about Romania (which the Romanians also tell about the Hungarians): The Hungarian press runs a competition, for which the third prize is a two-week holiday in Romania. The second prize is a one-week holiday in Romania. The first prize is that you don't have to go to Romania at all.

I find the not-having-to-go bit particularly appealing, as my last convalescence trip was after child number three was born, having had three caesareans in three years, and my obstetrician told my husband to take me away somewhere to recover. My husband announced proudly that he had found the perfect trip to pamper me and recharge my batteries: a week-long husky-dog sledding safari in northern Lapland, sleeping at night in reindeer-skin tents, and spending five hours a day clamping yourself, rigid with cold and fear, to the edge of a sled in minus 20 degrees with a blizzard lashing your face, shouting "mush mush" as the sled rattles, flies and bangs across rutted ice, you clinging on for dear life, while presumably all your stitches burst open but you are too cold to notice.

I had only been married three years, and was very much in love, so I gamely bought the polar sleeping bags, the first aid kit and the thermal underwear and weaned the baby. Then, and God is truly merciful and looks after his children, the day before departure, my back went into spasm and I could move neither arm nor leg. "Darling," I said to my husband with a huge grin, "you will have to go on my convalescence trip without me."

He came back after one week, and as I cut him free

from the same clothes he had left in a week earlier, he said three days would probably have been enough; adding that I might not have enjoyed it as he shared the tent with five Swiss engineers, none of whom changed so much as their socks for the whole week, and the tent already smelt a little high before they moved in...

Convalescence trips arranged by husbands are best imagined and not actually gone on. If by any chance my husband does book the Maldives, I will most likely go with him, though, as I am a good sport and always ready to give him another chance.

On the bright side, one of our dogs was spayed two days before my surgery, and her convalescence was ten days in a cage in the kitchen, with a funnel-shaped collar around her neck to stop her licking her wound, so things could be worse.

In fact, I did go on a convalescence trip. My brilliant husband in the end knew just what I really wanted, even if I didn't. Discarding all thoughts of the Maldives and the Caribbean, we went to a tiny, deserted Italian skiing resort – I use the word "resort" in a spirit of generosity – which was closing for the season due to a lack of snow and the total apathy of its slightly inbred mountain inhabitants.

There was basically just us and a bunch of tipsy ski-lift operators. For the last week, there was also a group of bewildered-looking Israelis with their rabbi, trying to celebrate Passover, wandering around and looking (in vain) for anything that looked like a boutique or a pizzeria that was open, as the mountain closed at two o'clock, and the village looked like a cemetery. Goodness knows which benighted travel agent sent them there – the lawyers will be sharpening their pencils.

For the last few days there was also a jolly English family group that was bussed in every day from an even more remote and inbred hamlet, displaying cheerful bulldog spirit and determined to enjoy themselves. The father's main job was to make sure the group of teenagers got back on the bus at the end of the day and didn't wander off with the rabbi or the tipsy ski-lift operators. There is nothing quite so deaf as an English teenager – "Tom, Tom, TOM, TOMMM!!!" shouted the father, as he sailed overhead on the chairlift while Tom was sitting with his headphones on, on the snow below. "Where is Will, Will? WILLLL, WWWIIILLLLL!!!"

At this, Tom gazed vacantly up at his receding parent as he disappeared, still bawling instructions, beyond the next pylon, from whence one could hear faint shreds of, "Tell Mum I have got Sam with me, tell Mum… TELL MUMMMM…." But there was no other visible reaction from Tom. Or perhaps he was Will, in which case, where was Tom…

Then there was the "Festa della Chiusura" to celebrate the last day on the mountain. A leggy blonde in a mini-skirt and furry boots pole-danced on top of a rapidly melting pirate ship made of snow, while a DJ played to a small crowd of snowboarders, pretty girls and elderly but still lecherous ex-ski instructors and everyone got happily drunk. One of the pretty girls sat in a deckchair with her head between her knees, quietly vomiting and claiming altitude sickness, while Tom and Will looked on in admiration.

The sun blazed down, the pistes were totally empty, the hot flushes meant I could ski in a T-shirt, and then the snow turned to slush, birds twittered, daisies, violets and heather covered the meadows below, and it was utter bliss.

This is why I love my husband. He knew that nothing could have been more perfect.

Honey, I shrunk the tumour

As I have mentioned, before I had even finished my chemo, my huge lump had retreated to a measly group of tiny sub-lumps. One of my friends said, not entirely jokingly, "It took one look at you and your conviction that you do things better than anyone else, and decided it didn't have a chance." Other people have asked for my green juice recipe. My Catholic Bavarian friends said that it was the Virgin Mary at the Church of Altötting, at whose shrine they had lit candles. My Greek relatives said it was St Ilias, whose icon they had hung round my neck; chosen because he is a relatively unknown and not very busy saint with only minor miracles on his CV, so he could therefore give me his undivided attention.

My ship-owner grandfather, back in 1914, hung up a votive offering of a silver model of a freight ship within the monastery on Ithaca, to commemorate its miraculous survival when a German U-boat had tried to torpedo it. The crew had prayed to their madonna who had ensured that the torpedo swerved at the last minute and missed the ship. I ought really to hang a silver model of a bosom next to it, but my grandfather was a very solemn, old-fashioned family patriarch, and I am not sure he would be thrilled at the juxtaposition.

In a more secular vein, no pun intended, my oncologist claims the credit for my tumour shrinking, due to his skilful use of intravenous drugs. Personally, I hold great store by my daily foraging for sorrel and nasturtium blossoms in the garden and heroic consumption of vast quantities of kale and broccoli, and most importantly, my refusal to do anything that stressed me. I also believe that keeping a good-humoured journal has been a huge help – you get into the habit of looking forward to every day, to every treatment, test or appointment with the same sense of excitement as a fisherman who casts his line afresh in a new pool each day: perhaps this day will offer up some comic gem, some fat fish, to add to the collection. Every day is a virgin field to harvest for a laugh. Most importantly, you are taking control of the raw material of your life. Like a sculptor kneading clay, you are shaping a mass of heavy stuff into a pleasing form, something that you can even put in a kiln and turn into something useful.

I am not alone it seems; one day during radiotherapy, I mentioned to Dee, one of the nurses, that I was writing a blog. "Oh," said Dee. "I had a lovely lady in a few years ago who was writing one as well. One day, she was lying on the radio bed, just like you, and I said something funny. She started laughing quite normally, but then her laughter became uncontrollable. I mean, what I had said was funny, but not *that* funny, so I got a bit worried she was becoming hysterical. A week later, she showed me her blog, where she confessed that she had actually wet her pants laughing, right there on the radiotherapy bed, but hadn't dared tell us."

I had often wondered why they place a paper towel under you on the radiotherapy bed. Now I can see. "It's better than crying," as Dee said very wisely.

I do occasionally have guilt feelings about how lucky I am so far, but when I mentioned this to my oncologist, he said he didn't think anyone with cancer was particularly lucky, but if I was worried, I could have some Counselling.

The dentist

In his goody-bag of little pills that he can prescribe after the main chemotherapy has ended, Prof E has got some bio-phosphides which are good for bones and help stop baby cancer cells in their tracks. It can also cause necrotising jaw disease if you have to have dental surgery while taking it, so I was dispatched to the dentist for clearance.

The dentist took some X-rays, saying, laughingly, "I would be very surprised if you needed a tooth pulled out." He then looked at the X-rays and said, "Hmm, I think you need to have a tooth pulled out. Please go and have a 3D imaging X-ray tomorrow."

At the X-ray centre, there was another *Alice in Wonderland* moment when the radiologist said, "Have you had the tooth I am going to X-ray taken out?"

"No," I said, bewildered. "It is still in there and you are going to X-ray it."

She then said patiently, as if talking to a rather slow child, "Yes, but what I am asking is if you have ever had it extracted?"

Did she mean taken out and then put back? I didn't dare ask, and this could clearly have gone on for a while, so I gave in and just said that no, I hadn't ever had it taken out. I still don't know what she meant. Necrotising brain disease.

The graduation ceremony

Following the initial analogy where I imagined a visit to Cancerland as a cruise to a new continent, this is the equivalent of the goodbye dinner at the captain's table on the last night of the trip, before disembarking in the home port.

Greeks are a very hospitable people, and when a guest leaves someone's home, it is traditional to offer a ceremonial farewell feast, often based around a rice platter (pilaf) with lots of delicacies. My father used to call this the *"Asikhtir pilaf"* which roughly translates as "The fuck-off pilaf".

It feels right that, after a long treatment, some formal marking of the end should take place. Any goal, once achieved, can leave you feeling flat and purposeless, no matter how much the achievement of the goal has been longed for. The clinic offers a day of talks and discussions and tips, with a nice lunch, to ease patients back into daily life and wean them off the clinic support system, so that they don't ghost around like the Phantom of the Opera, unable to sever the ties and turning up like bad pennies wanting blood tests and scans. The *"Asikhtir pilaf"* is a wise and kind graduation ceremony.

The meaning of life

I did once know the meaning of life, but sadly I then forgot what it was. It was whispered to me by a babbling brook in a forest in upstate New York when I was an art student, walking on a sunny autumn day in the woods all ablaze with colours of gold with a group of other art students. We had eaten too many magic mushrooms – we didn't really know what we were doing, and were well away. The birds spoke to us, the breeze showered colours on us, the shafts of sunlight fragmented into shards of diamonds and sapphires, and as I knelt by its luminously glowing mossy bank and put my ear to it, a brook of liquid crystal told me that the meaning of life was... I am damned if I can remember... I would have made a terrible Shaman: "O hear this all you tribes folk!! The gods have spoken to me, and they say, the gods say... um, yes, the gods *did* say something, now what was it they said, it is on the tip of my tongue; I know there is something I am supposed to tell you; aarrghh, no, it's gone, I can't remember a thing. Not the foggiest idea. It's really gone. Oh well, can you all come back tomorrow? Yes, you will need to bring more sacrificial cockerels. You can take any that are still alive back home with you, just purify them overnight and bring them back tomorrow. So sorry, mushroom brain..."

As it turns out, a year of having cancer has given me an unexpected second chance at glimpsing the meaning of life – one probably better founded than the previous one, and best of all, one I can remember.

Our tragedy is that we don't learn important things like taking time for friends and family, letting go of things, accepting help and love, giving it back, until we are taken by the scruff of the neck, pressed violently up against a wall with our head being banged several times.

This can be what a diagnosis of illness is like. We are forced to pause, to reassess, to see that most things carry on very well without us, and that, in the end, the glitter of life is just that, passing glitter, and that true gold is found in family, friends, love and laughter, as those Harvard researchers found.

I can honestly say that my year of having cancer was one of the happiest of my life, where I finally understood so many crucial things to which I had been oblivious or to which I had attached no importance: having a peaceful routine focusing on health rather than acquiring things, cooking in an engaged and leisurely way, rather than juggling three pans of burning stuff while cradling the phone under my ear, reading whole books, seeing friends for no particular reason, properly listening to people rather than putting the phone on hands-free and trying to answer emails at the same time, walking somewhere rather than rushing in a car and getting bad-tempered, writing a journal rather than writing reports, not having permanent back-ache from sitting at a desk, giving quieter or shyer people the time and room to blossom in front of me, appreciating small things, just being kind.

Rather like fracking, it seems to me that huge ground reserves of a rich fuel lie just under the surface of our lives, waiting for us to tap into them – vast streams of strength and love that are there for the taking.

Living in a bubble of love gives greater happiness than any of the glittering prizes offer, and for this belated insight,

I am profoundly grateful to my long-suffering family and friends, and to cancer.

I don't think this is what the brook whispered to me in that upstate New York forest all ablaze with gold and flames, but, to be honest, who in their right minds takes lessons on the meaning of life from a babbling brook? I hope that I never forget that initial wave of peace and acceptance that washed over me on my small Greek island when I was first told I had two to five years to live, and I also hope that it will wash over me again when my tide really does, one day, go out.

PART TWO

Metastasis

FALSE ALARM, MANY APOLOGIES, I thought I had finished this journal with the previous nicely-judged final paragraph. Life is not always as elegant as art, and it turns out that, in spite of being a straight A student with impeccable blood-test results and glowing reports from all my doctors, I didn't manage to graduate. Failed. Repeat the year, probably never graduate, be an eternal student, like one of those aging PhD graduates who go on for ever and ever and whose supervisor retires before they are finished. No *Asikhtir pilaf*, no jokes about "Hope we never see you again." My cancer had metastasised bafflingly fast, while I was still having treatment first time around in fact. You can imagine what that felt like. *"What? I can't have metastasised so soon. I only finished chemo six months ago. You mean that all that time while I was doing so brilliantly and getting top marks, the cancer has spread all over my liver and is now not operable? You cannot be serious???"*

But they are serious. They avoid eye contact, they look away, they say things like "I am very sorry" and "Prof E will talk to you when he gets back from his conference in Chicago."

This is not how my journal was supposed to continue. It was so nicely arranged into beginning, middle and end, a clear tourist map, not this messy *terra incognita* with no outlines, and pictures of winds and dragons in the corners where the topographers weren't sure what to draw.

I am back in Cancerland, this time as a resident, not a tourist.

Pitch-perfect

Before my metastasis, flattered by the obligatory praise from my friends, I thought about getting this journal published, with proceeds going to a cancer charity. I got rather excited about it; I was planning my appearances on *Woman's Hour* on BBC Radio 4, and I pestered my friend Laura, a literary agent, until she sent it off to a couple of colleagues. They all agreed in tones of faint moral disapproval that, as I had myself *admitted*, I was not a single mother on benefits with small children, nor struggling to hold down a job, had no immediate financial worries, had a loving husband, nice friends and, worst of all, private health insurance. The final, unspoken reproach was that I was not even very sick, and therefore "the manuscript has sadly no commercial appeal."

Now, however, as someone with a *very serious disease*, I thought I might have a better chance of success. The trick, I realised, was to pitch it much more cunningly…

"Ileana von Hirsch was happily married with grown-up children a great job, lots of friends and private health insurance. Her life was perfect, or so she thought, till one day, she woke up to find she had incurable cancer."

That should simply *fly* off the shelves. I have not spent 20 years in marketing for nothing.

Thus emboldened, I thought I would continue my journal.

Ileana's adventures in Cancerland

It all started a few weeks after I had finished radiation. I woke up one morning with a sharp pain in my shoulder and a fever. A weekend of course. A quick search on the internet – "pain in right shoulder and fever" – brought up the clear diagnosis of gall stones, so on Monday I went to see Dr H.

Dr H looks and sounds like Bagheera, the smooth-as-silk panther in *The Jungle Book*. Like all top doctors, he loves it when patients self-diagnose on Google, and turn up in his clinic with an overnight hospital bag already packed and tell him exactly what is wrong with them. He is so grateful to them, and to Google; I can tell as I am very sensitive to other people.

"Fine," he said, "if you say it is gall bladder, let's get you scanned." Four hours later the scans showed that my gall bladder was pristine, but the imaging doctor suggested further investigations. Dr H had just got back from his annual month in India, volunteering in a village clinic where they don't have scanning machines or imaging doctors, and no one Googles their symptoms, a sort of pre-lapsarian garden of medicinal Eden. Dr H clearly yearns for the simpler times. "I really don't think that further scans are necessary," he said in a very dismissive way, "They wouldn't do them in my Indian village. They would just send the person home with a bag of herbs and he would go back to work in the fields and stop worrying, and would be fine. We worry too much and over-think things. Here, in the west, we are ruled by our technology, and have forgotten about nature."

Wise as Dr H is, I was still hoping for a little technology rather than a bag of herbs, so I kept quiet in what I hoped was a very multicultural and non-judgemental way. Dr

H studied the scan report a few moments longer, then – and here one can only be grateful that his years of western training took over – he said, "Well, perhaps it would be best to have a further look." So back I went to the hospital that afternoon.

I have to bless Dr H for that further investigation. My liver was a mess. "Shadows, lesions, diffusion," and other words floated in the air. The hepatology consultant who had been called in looked at me and said solemnly, avoiding prolonged eye contact, "Given your history, this is likely to be cancer again. I am so sorry. Your oncologist will tell you more. Good luck."

It is wonderful to see the medical establishment swing into action – within 24 hours, I had been scanned from brain to toe, tagged and admitted to hospital, and a team of oncologists and consultants formed. Dr H came by to see me, very sweet of him, given that I was not exactly an ornament to his Indian Village Concept – "Why are you doing this to me?" he said, "You are supposed to be all cured and of no further interest." I apologised very humbly and said I was sorry. Dr H has a lugubrious bedside manner; he has learned not to offer me Counselling, but cannot totally control himself.

"There will be times when you will feel like crying, so I am going to give you a book of gentle and meditative poems, edited by Daisy Goodwin, which when you are feeling depressed you can dip into and they will offer you solace."

I told him that I couldn't think of anything worse, and promised to send him my own book which would, I hope, cheer him up. He looked doubtful. "There is lots about you in it," I offered encouragingly, which just elicited a Bagheera-type growl.

The next visit to my hospital bed was from a consultant oncologist (Prof E was away at a breast cancer conference again in the US), trailing a white-coated, comet tail of juniors and resident oncologists holding notebooks. I had never had a team of doctors before, and I began to grasp that my status in the hospital was changing in a rather gratifying way.

Dr C exuded bonhomie and jolliness. "So," he said rubbing his hands, "your cancer has metastasised, rather quicker than anyone expected, especially as you did so well last year, but the thing to focus on is that we know exactly what to do about it, we have wonderful drugs. We call it 'living with Cancer', which hopefully we will get you to do for as long as possible." He looked so happy that I felt no doubt that all would happen just as he said. I cannot recommend denial highly enough as a policy for getting through awkward patches in life.

A mental adjustment must now be made – one no longer talks about a cure, one talks about management, with the aim of drawing out as many years of comfortable, high-quality life as possible. Unless, of course, one gets run over by a bus or blown up somewhere – thoughts I find strangely relaxing, as it goes to show that there is no point worrying: anyone of us could shuffle off our mortal coil, or be yanked out of it, at any moment, cancer or no cancer.

Sometime in 1994 or thereabouts, my husband and I booked a trip to Egypt. A week before we were due to leave, there was a huge terrorist attack on a couple of major tourist sites on the Nile, and we duly called in at the Egyptian consulate to get travel advice. The small, courteous official looked at us and said with great simplicity, "If Allah has decided that your time has come, it will be so, and if not, then it will not be so." Quite.

It did strike me that I was lucky that all this had been discovered the day before I was due to fly to Greece. I could just imagine the look on the face of the local radiographer if he had had to see me again – "What! Are you still here? I thought you would be dead by now!"

Life as a high-status metastasis

Oh boy, can you now hold your head up high as a deeply cool Metastasis rather than a Boring Breast! You are finally one of the cool gang, the hard-core cancer posse. The scans and appointments are all now pleasingly familiar and I no longer feel like a lost girl at a new school, but more like a prefect, a position to which I had always aspired in vain – I never made it beyond ink monitor in my entire school career, which, as ink-wells had been dispensed with a few years before, was not as grand as it sounded. It was better than nothing, though, and I swelled with pride when I was appointed.

My hospital admission for my first key PET scan was chaotic for some reason, surely nothing to do with Dr H's method of queue-barging for his patients.

"This is Dr H. I would like you to admit my patient Mrs Ileana von Hirsch to ward six right now." Voice of receptionist explaining that there were no beds.

"Nevertheless, I am sure you can find a bed for Mrs von

Hirsch and I will be sending her over in five minutes to be admitted."

Voice of girl in a slightly higher pitch this time explaining that she couldn't do that. She doesn't know Dr H. "Excellent, so Mrs von Hirsch will come over right now. I would also like her to have a scan at 12pm with Dr Patel."

Voice of girl at an even higher pitch explaining that there were no scan slots available and especially not with Dr Patel.

"I understand, but I know that Dr Patel will be able to do it, so I will fill out the form and send it over with Mrs von Hirsch now."

No more voice of girl to be heard at any pitch at all.

"Do go over to the hospital now, they are expecting you," says Dr H to me.

———————————

By the time I had been admitted to the hospital, ward six, I was very late for my 12pm scan slot with Dr Patel. As a new girl, I would have got told off and sent to the back of the queue. This year, the nurse – who clearly has dealt with Dr H before – took my elbow and whispered, "Follow my lead and don't look surprised, I am going to squeeze you in, don't worry about all that hospital gown nonsense, just slip in here and don't let them see you." She pointed to a young girl and her grandfather who were sitting quietly, waiting. "They are next in line," she said, "but I am giving you their slot."

Then, turning to the girl, she said a breezy and insincere "Won't be a minute! We are just setting it up for you."

"But PET scans are 45 minutes aren't they?" I whispered,

as I was doing a furtive and lightning-swift change into a hospital gown behind the door.

"Yes," whispered back the nurse, grinning, "I am a bit of a Pinocchio today," and she pulled a long nose movement. I thought this was a little mean, but, when one is high-status, low-status people just have to wait patiently as I used to have to.

I was in and out of that machine like a dose of salts – all normal decorum and box-ticking requirements abandoned. The scanner was equipped with a speaking guide who tells you in an American accent what to do and when to breathe. The switch was turned to the fastest setting, so the voice was squeaking at helium-balloon speed: "Breathe in, breathe out, breathe in, breathe out," while I, totally unable to keep up, and always at least three breaths behind, was starting to hyperventilate. We managed, however, the Voice of America and I, and in record time I was ejected, exhausted and panting for breath from the scanner. I gave it a pat on the shoulder, respect where due, and made my way back to where the girl and her grandfather were sitting. The grandfather was then taken in, the girl giving him a last kiss and I hoped that they had remembered to set the voice dial back to its normal stately pace. The grandfather didn't look well enough for the speed-breathing race.

The granddaughter sat with wet eyes, sniffing, then turned to me and said, "Is it as scary as people say?"

I told her the story of my first scary scan and how she shouldn't listen to other people's horror stories, so she dried her eyes. I touched her on the arm and said with a delicacy that was unusual for me, "I am sure that your father will be fine."

"He is not my father," she said wearily, "he is my husband; we've been married for 12 years." There was no coming back from that for me, so I wished her good luck and left.

Getting a second chemo port put in is boringly familiar. I remember having a superstitious pang when my first chemo port was removed after my original surgery. A little voice had whispered in my head, "Wouldn't it be better to just leave it in for a year, just in case?" The old umbrella principle – if you take an umbrella, it won't rain; if you don't, it will. Always listen to those little voices in your head even if it worries doctors (actually, it is best not to admit to doctors that you hear little voices in your head).

My first new chemo had to be done immediately with a needle in the back of the hand, before I had time to get a new port put in, and after half an hour that felt like an entire morning of searching for veins and husbands fainting and general wailing, the nurses gave up trying to get the needle in, and, to everyone's relief, sent me back to hospital to get a chemo port put in urgently so they could continue the chemo without me gouging their eyes out. It was a Friday afternoon and the hastily summoned surgeon appeared in the operating theatre, out of breath and wearing a flowery shirt and Bermuda shorts, looking rather confused. "I am supposed to be on the M40 going away for the weekend," he explained rather sheepishly. "So, we are putting a PICC line in are we?"

"No," I said, "a chemo port..." Lucky I am an old hand and know what is going on.

"Ah, OK, no problem, have you fasted for the last six hours?"

"Yes," I lied. No way was I not going to have the port put in.

"OK, let's get going then. A little scratch, and count to ten…"

One can overdo the "high status helpful prefect" bit, as I discovered one day in chemo. In the cubicle opposite me was a very anxious older lady who had come in for the first day of a new chemo treatment for breast cancer that had metastasised. She was essentially following in my footsteps, so the kind clinic nurse said to her, "I will get that nice lady opposite you (i.e. me) to tell you her experiences so you aren't so worried." I leapt out of my chair, unplugged my chemo trolley and rushed over to her – almost indecent in my haste to share my expertise. Before she had time to collect her wits, I had delivered myself of my entire stock of wisdom, and then retired back to my cubicle feeling pleased at my good deed. Later, I heard the lady say to the clinic nurse, "Could I please change my chemo dates and come on Mondays from now on?"

Science Ed 1

My new and dizzyingly fast promotion up the cancer league is going very satisfyingly – not only am I now a Metastasised Liver, I am also a medical curiosity in that my cancer phenotype has changed from Her2 negative to

Her2 positive. This only happens in 5% of the Cancerland population, and means that I get discussed in the cancer clinic weekly meetings where all the consultants gather to brainstorm about their interesting cases. It also means that my cancer is much easier to treat, but that is almost beside the point when one is on a celebrity roll.

The first thing that you notice as a high-status metastasis is that you are suddenly on first-name terms with your oncologists, and that you have a team of them rather than just one – this is hugely gratifying for attention-seekers like myself and I can feel it going to my head already. "My oncology team" sounds so much more important than "My oncologist". As with a Formula One racer, as opposed to a Formula Four one, the pit stops are now full of highly skilled experts milling around in a state of excitement, rather than a single mechanic servicing several drivers at the same time. The second thing you notice– and this is a little frightening – is that you are listened to. You suggest a scan rather sooner than they were planning, and they say yes straight away. You wonder out loud whether your heart is fluttering, and an echogram is fixed for the next day. You are asked whether you actually want the chemo – this is taking it a bit too far – "No," you cry, "I am a Libra, I don't really know as much as I pretend, in fact, I know nothing at all, so please don't ask me to make any important decisions. Toss a coin if you aren't sure! Just don't make me decide."

The most interesting upgrade by far, though, is that now you are considered to be a valuable part of the whole treatment plan; people explain things to you in more detail as it is exciting even for them in a way which it was not previously. All residents of Cancerland are offered a basic education in science. Not a very thorough one, but it does help to make the whole experience infinitely more interesting, so I recommend taking the course.

Prof E, for example, explains how easy my new cancer is to treat by balling up his hand into a fist and sticking three pencils between his fingers, hedgehog fashion, to represent a cancer molecule and its three Her2 positive receptors. It is rather like the child's game of "This little piggy went to market", except it goes, "This little pencil gets attacked by this targeted drug. This little pencil gets attacked by this targeted drug, and this little pencil cries *wee wee wee* all the way home."*

It is a joy to be receiving a sophisticated education at my age. Interestingly Science Ed 1 is a recent development. In Greece, cancer is still called the *"Amilitos"* which means the sickness that can't be mentioned. Even doctors don't like naming it. My friend Rachel's father had no idea he was seeing an oncologist in Athens or even had brain cancer until his daughter arrived from the UK and put things in order. This is a real shame. Knowing why the smallest little piggy cried *wee wee wee all the way home* is very empowering.

For those who have never quite got to grips with the jargon that gets thrown at you, unless you are in Greece, in which case no one tells you anything anyway, here are my Science Ed. 1 course notes on what is – or isn't – growing in you:

---

* I should make it clear that these are my words, not Prof E's.

Tumour – any cell can become cancerous, just as any child can turn bad – nature or nurture – a bit of both, who knows… A tumour, or carcinoma, is a critical mass of hooligans that have turned into a gang.

Tumour sizes are graded T1 to T4, with various subsections – in gang terms, 1 is the smallest and weediest, 4 the biggest in town (This and the next two points are where it gets competitive).

The different grades indicate how far a cancerous cell differs from the norm, or what it should be, i.e. how much worse the individual gang member is from the model citizen he should be. Grades are from 1 to 4, with 1 being OK for community service, 2 being suspended sentence, 3 being eligible for parole one day, and 4 being a real bad-ass, throw him in jail and never let him out.

The bad-ass Carcinoma Gang

Stages – these indicate how far the cancer has spread; again, it's on a scale of 1 to 4, with 1 being a very local gang that can be killed off with one attack, and 4 meaning it has spread into other 'hoods and just has to be contained by vigilant policing in the hope that it won't get too out of control.

Primary – the original cancer; can be one type. Small-time burglary, for example.

Metastatic – secondary cancer which has developed from the primary one. This can be another type. Drugs and prostitution. The gang members often separate and go underground to infiltrate further, and don't always swagger around in a group. Can take a while to identify.

Histology – the microanatomy of the cancer cell, i.e. what kind it is, which will determine your treatment. Tells you whether to go after this gang with wailing sirens or by stealth.

Receptors – these are little tentacles that stick out of a cell like Prof E's pencils stuck between his knuckles. The type of cancer you have and the treatment for it will depend on what these receptors react with.

Cancer cells "express" what type they are. This doesn't mean that they are artists trying to paint or write poetry; it describes their microanatomy – e.g. what receptors stick out and provide targets for oncologists to attack the nucleus inside the cell.

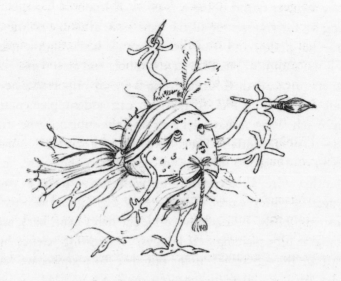

A most expressive cancer cell

Once you have mastered these terms, you can also impress your oncologist by researching cancer trials and telling him which one you think he ought to put you on as he clearly doesn't know as much as you do.

This needs careful handling and an unusual amount of tact. You don't want him to flannel you with a lot of "There, there, of course you don't understand, don't worry your brain about it"; but you don't want him to think you are a panic-stricken pest who is going to send newspaper clippings to him three times a week in case he hasn't heard what the science editor of the *Daily Telegraph* has been told by a mate in a pub the night before…

Ideally, you should download all the research papers (or

get a clever friend doing a masters at Imperial College to log on for you, as not all the papers are available online to the hoi polloi) and read them through while highlighting all the technical bits that have symbols and acronyms. You then print all this out and put it in an important, new, medical-looking file. To this you can add supplementary research that you have done around the subject – the trial doctors' credentials, your microbiologist cousin's input, who made the test tubes, what kind of mice they were, how fat they were. Then you must bring the file with you to your meeting with the prof, displaying the highlighted acronyms ostentatiously. Be casually confident here. Lean back and look at him piercingly. If he says, "Interesting science but still at the lab stage", point out that 20 people have had the drug as well as umpteen fat mice. He will look at you admiringly.

This strategy had exactly the desired effect when I tried it out on Prof E. It was, I figured, very unlikely that he had heard about this particular trial as he doesn't have time to read the *Daily Telegraph*, what with all the conferences he goes to and the other oncologists he has to meet. I was quite right.

Prof E looked impressed and said, "You are a most unusual patient", skimmed over my pages of yellow high-light, and then explained why I hadn't understood anything. But he did refer me to a colleague of his, Prof J, who glories in the title of "Speciality-Novelty Drugs", which reminded me uncomfortably of a bad period with one of my sons and deliveries from the internet in unmarked yellow padded envelopes.

Prof E's referring letter to his colleague read, "Mrs von

Hirsch is a very articulate woman," which is of course encrypted doctor-code. Referral letters are all coded:

- "This very nice patient" means you can take her on, no problem, she doesn't argue and her insurance pays on time.
- "This lady is not to be trifled with" means take her on at your risk.
- "This patient is concerned about..." means that she is a nervous wreck and needs a lot of soothing talk.
- "This lady is very articulate" means that you can't say, "There, there don't worry your brain about it" and expect her to say nothing.
- "She would like reassurance" means, for God's sake, don't open any new cans of worms.
- "Unusual symptoms with unclear pathological cause" means she is a raving hypochondriac.
- "Mrs S is a very inquisitive lady..." – my friend Afreen had this – it means she will drive you mad with lots of questions. Book her a long appointment.
- "I look forward to hearing your thoughts" means call me the minute she has left the room so I can explain...

And they think we don't realise...

The second opinion and Science Ed 2

Prof J has clearly been brought onto the team on a "keep Ileana quiet" basis, which is fine by me, I am more than happy to be reassured that everything is fine and that we have investigated everything that needs investigating. I just hope that he doesn't start on about giving up meat and sugar and eating more kale. I did that last year: look where it got me.

As the "Novelty Drugs" specialist, on the Mount Olympus of Oncology, he is right up there with Zeus. Like all great men, he was very natural and open. "Fascinating trial you asked me to look into," he said, "I know one of the guys doing it, but hadn't heard about it. I made some notes, but I have to say I found it quite heavy-going, I hope I understood it all…" Then he proceeded to draw all over his notes, little pictures of cancer cells and microphages, blood vessels, hormone sensitive receptors. Arrows pierced them, lines flew around them, and acronyms, furiously circled, were stamped on top of it all. It was rather like spending an hour sitting in the cockpit of a jet fighter, with an ace pilot doing loop-the-loops, firing guns, dropping bombs and showing you how he used the controls – totally exhilarating; you think you understand everything, and then as soon as you leave the room and start to formulate what to tell your husband, all you can remember is that there was an amazing guy sitting in a cockpit with a steering-wheel.

One piece of information I do distinctly remember is that, when I asked him about diets, he said that there was nothing wrong with the odd chocolate biscuit and that there was absolutely no science behind any of the diets that excluded any food groups. "Eat well" is the answer, and don't get fat, as this produces hormones, which Breasts like me shouldn't ever have again. I asked him to put this into his follow-up letter to show the food police back home.

The only other thing I remember is that, in spite of being an ace fighter pilot at the controls of an F35, he couldn't use the photocopier on his desk and had to call the nurse in to do it.

Shortly after this, I was chatting to Prof E about my treatment programme and what Prof J had said. "Did he tell you about TDM-1s?" asked Prof E.

"No," I said, "What are they?"

Prof E beamed and, to my joy, he began balling his hand up into a fist again, this time sticking imaginary pencils between the knuckles. I held my breath so as not to break the spell as Oncology – part 2 (advanced students) was hoving into view. "Ah," he said, "they are a fabulous drug that I was lucky enough to be involved in developing. They are basically small nuclear bombs that we attach to a drug that sticks to a tumour receptor to break its way into the cell, and then, BOOM!!! The nuclear bit goes off and blows it all to smithereens."

His eyes were now shining with pleasure and I suddenly had a flashing image of him as a small boy in his parents' garage back in Auckland, making home-made bombs and other IEDs and blowing things up. It could really have gone either way with him: armed robber, arsonist, terrorist, oncologist… His parents must have been mightily relieved that he chose oncology.

"Sounds fabulous!" I enthused. "Can I have some of those TDMs? Can I blow things up into smithereens too?"

Prof E came back to earth with a start, wiped his glasses and adjusted his collar. "No," he said, "you can't. They are only for me to play with. You can only have them if, and when, we need to go nuclear."

So that is something nice to look forward to at least.

BOOOOOOMMMM…

Prof E, aged nine – it could have gone either way with him

A small reality check

If you think that it is now all about you, which you might be forgiven for thinking, I should put you straight.

My first few days after the diagnosis of metastasis were spent trying to stop the weeping and wailing from friends, family and colleagues. This is understandable; I make the same mistake even now: when I hear someone has cancer, I think, "Poor thing, they are dead," even though I know from my own situation that this is completely wrong and only the ignorant would think that. Cancer has such a bad name, it is the victim of its own reputation, and nothing it does can really persuade people that it is not always the bad boy it appears to be. I feel like starting a campaign to reha-bilitate it and integrate it back into society – get it a good job, register it for jury duty, and have it start paying taxes. Until then your job is to keep the troops calm which leaves you no time to feel sorry for yourself.

The worst are of course the Greeks who have drama and tragedy, rhetoric and hyperbole in their DNA. I remember one summer on Ithaca as a child, when the Greek army was mobilised in response to unacceptable incursions by the Turks in the Aegean. In spite of many common inter-ests and shared cultural features, Greco-Turkish relations have been fractious since the fall of Constantinople in 1453. Nothing whips a Greek up into a frenzy as fast as dust-up with a Turk – a fact not lost on both Greek and Turkish politicians. So, in the middle of an idyllic, lazy summer, the young men of the island were suddenly summoned to report to barracks on the mainland and our converted fishing boat was requisitioned for defence purposes (even though Ithaca shares a sea with Italy rather than Turkey, and it would have taken our eight-metre boat about a week to cross over to the Aegean). As my cold-blooded, practical Austrian mother wrote to her mother in Canada:

Mama, you can't imagine what is going on here. Panos [my father] is running around frothing at the mouth with a dagger in his hand, saying he is going to kill any Turk that gets lost badly enough to end up on Ithaca, and I am afraid he is going to fall over and hurt himself. We went down to the ferry to wave the boys away who were going to war, and all the women of the island were down on the jetty dressed in black, tearing their hair out and wailing, but not ONE of them had thought to give the boys a sandwich.

In the end, the boys arrived at the barracks to find that the army suppliers had managed to supply them with only left boots – who knows, perhaps the Turks had the right boots. They were all sent back again two days later, barefoot. Greeks in crisis are very special.

As a consequence of this love of drama, no Greek suffers illness on their own – there is always a retinue of friends and relatives sitting by them every day suffocating them with food, attention, love, tears, scoldings, second opinions, third opinions, homemade soups, fourth opinions, gossip, phone calls, arguments with children/ex-spouses/in-laws, bureaucratic nightmares, elegies for the already departed.

While I like attention, I like peace and quiet and carrying on as normal as well. Until one is dead, one is really *not dead*, so to speak.

My Greek partner, Evi, immediately offered to come and stay with me when she heard my cancer had metastasised. "No, please don't," I begged, in alarm. "You must stay at least a three-hour flight away from me – Athens is a good place."

Evi is used to me after 20 years of partnership and has learned not to be offended by my cold, English temperament. "But I am an excellent person to have on hand when friends are sick," she said, "I am a tower of strength and can look after you. Remember how I practically moved in when X had cancer?" I did indeed, every scene and chapter and verse. I managed to persuade her that I didn't need a tower of strength, it was all very boring, and I wasn't dying, but were I to be dying she could come and stay with me.

The Pollyanna Personality Disorder

"*Pollyanna* is a best-selling 1913 novel by Eleanor H Porter that is now considered a classic of children's literature, with the title character's name becoming a popular term for someone with the same very optimistic outlook. Also, the subconscious bias towards the positive is often described as the *Pollyanna* principle." What Wikipedia doesn't realise is that this is not a principle, but a genuine psychological disorder.

I loved the *Pollyanna* books as a child and cried buckets over Pollyanna's travails, wondering how on earth anyone could possibly stay so resolutely positive through the most testing times. Pollyanna's characteristic was to always find things to be glad about. I now realise that I suffer from the same personality disorder as she did – the Pollyanna Personality Disorder (PPD). I am incapable of contemplating anything negative, the brain just will not accept any adverse imprints other than the shallowest and most fleeting ones, and those only survive a few minutes before disappearing in a puff of electro-magnetic explosions. The unnatural "chill end of the spectrum" as Prof E put it early on.

There is in fact some science behind my PPD theory – we know that the left hemisphere of our brains is responsible for shaping all the data experienced by the right hemisphere into a story or narrative. My left hemisphere has the happy knack of only telling cheerful stories. The opposite is true of depressives, who can have CBT to help retrain their left hemispheres to look on the bright side. We PPD sufferers would never dream of CBT to teach us to look on the glum side.

I wonder if Prof J would start a clinical trial on the effect on survival rates for cancer patients with PPD compared to those with normal brains. I am sure that the results would be astonishing, and something else for us PPDs to be glad about.

"Do you think that this disorder is a problem for you?" asked my friend Laura over lunch – she is acting as literary agent for a life coach who is writing his memoirs, and is in full therapy mode.

I considered this for a moment. I had almost alienated a Greek friend, who felt that my cheerfulness was all a pretence, and that I was shutting her out of my world. My friend felt unfairly done out of a really meaty drama, so I had to invent lots of fearful and morbid thoughts that I could share with her. After that, she felt much better and cried and said she loved me. I cried too. Then I thought about whether it had been cathartic and whether I felt better, but it was impossible to say. The minute I put down the phone, my PPD burst into action and erased any memory of what I had managed to think of to tell her – too shallow an imprint on my brain. After this temporary interruption, my narrating hemisphere picked up its rosy-coloured story again, right where it had left off.

"Perhaps it is just very irritating for your friends and no worse than that," Laura eventually suggested, as I was silent for too long. I agreed with her that it was not a problem for me at all, but I was glad she had told me how irritating it was for others.

"Hmmmm," said Laura and focused on her panna cotta.

Spousal sympathetic symptom disorder

Apparently, this is not an uncommon reaction on the part of spouses.

Your husband, until now your rock and anchor, suddenly develops full-blown hypochondria. A slight cough, a pain in the side that persisted over a period of three weeks, would send my husband into a tail-spin. "You will have to bury me, I can tell this is the end, I am riddled with cancer." My first reaction was annoyance that I was going to have to stop thinking about myself and start thinking about others again. I am not proud of this, but as almost any wife and mother will know, putting oneself first is a novelty not to be relinquished without a fight.

An appointment was duly made with Dr H, who listened to Florian talk death and funerals and making a will. Dr H, to his credit – in the spirit of a man-to-man understanding of the seriousness of men's problems – didn't even mention his Indian Village Concept, and sent him straight off for a reassuring number of X-rays and scans; the results of which were unanimous in agreement that there was nothing that a little vigorous exercise wouldn't fix.

This was obviously an unacceptable outcome and there will inevitably be more tests. But I'm afraid I got there first, my husband is going to bury me, and there is no way he is wriggling out of that one, unless he very selfishly throws himself under a train. I am *glad* that I have cancer as Pollyanna would have said.

Prognosis and eternal life

Prognosis is the huge white elephant in the room; the only thing one does not Google, the only thing one does not ask the doctors, other than couched in convoluted terms, which elicits suitably convoluted answers such as, "We will be bitterly disappointed if you don't make five years" and "We are aiming at the stars with you."

In fact, and this is perhaps a hard thing for non-Cancerland residents to understand, an intimate bond with a finite end is something very peaceful and can be a source of contentment. Gone are the long-term worries, financial or familial, gone too are the vague projects that have loomed over your future like a cloud – no longer relevant, leave them to someone else. I have had a full life with plenty of good years; I am no teenager, desperate to experience life before it is snuffed out. At my age, living another 30 years means ending up lying in bed like a vegetable with Alzheimer's or Parkinson's and daytime television left on 24/7 in a corner of a room, which, as your glasses are out of reach and no one has thought of updating your prescription for six years, you can't see anyway. No, thank you. We Cancerland residents have a *Get out of jail* card up our sleeve. I truly can't see why people want to live for ever.

I recently had a conversation with a very rich Los Angeles friend who is in the queue for genetic engineering to arrest/reverse the aging process, and make him immortal. He did qualify his wish by saying he only wanted to live for ever on condition that he could continue to be himself; with shed-loads of money, houses on three continents, and a real babe as a girlfriend.

The prospect of living for ever with a whole lot of rich, permanently youthful and super-healthy Los Angelenos all watching their diet, going for genetic maintenance every six months, avoiding gluten and alkaline foods, and dealing with an extended family of about 200 – including the requisite quota of failed grandchildren/great-grand-children, great-great-grand-children, six or seven bitter ex-spouses (who stays married for 100 years?) and umpteen alimony payments, fills me with utter horror. On the other side of the coin, imagine the muddy masses – who will presumably include my children who couldn't afford the genetic upgrade, who will probably live the same way as battery chickens do now – inferior animals kept under virtual digital sedation in cubicles, and thinking they are happy. I tell my friend that, were I to have to live for another 100 years, my next business would be a check-out clinic where those bitterly rueing their decision to live for ever could come and put an end to it, having shot their ex-spouses and failed descendants.

A thoughtful German friend wrote to me to suggest that having cancer a second time round must be like falling downstairs when you had just got to the top. In a sense, yes, but it is far more like the myth of Sisyphus – rolling a heavy boulder up a hill only for it to fall back once he got it to the top. The ancient Greeks thought of this as a punishment, but Albert Camus knew better – *il faut imaginer Sisyphus heureux*. This is in fact all there is to life, one has to imagine Sisyphus happy just rolling the boulder, irrespective of results – that is his purpose – happiness lies in doing it well. It is totally unhelpful to think how different life could be if the boulder just for once stayed put and one could do something else. Life is just rolling your boulder along as well as possible. In fact, if you have no boulder of your own to roll, what on earth do you do all day long?

Living without long-term plans is rather like being a child again, when reaching the age of ten seemed as grown up as it could get – after that, the featureless prairie of old age stretched out into the heat haze. And, like a child, the heart becomes light again. I have never believed in the sanctity of human life – mine or anyone else's – as opposed to the sanctity of anything else on this planet, and this brings a sense of cosmic comfort – we are utterly unimportant in an impersonal universe, and nothing matters in the slightest. Stardust to stardust.

In short, the usual vocabulary of the battlefield when people talk about cancer is to me incomprehensible, I am not a fighter, it is not a struggle, I am not fighting my cancer, that would be like fighting myself. We are room-mates, we compromise and make each other laugh and agree on who does the dishes and who is cooking. It is more of a dance than a fight. We are going to live together till the end now, me and my C, so best to get on well and become very good friends – as long as it is clear who is the alpha around here and who takes the rubbish out.

Best friends – note the pencil-shaped Her2+ receptors…
I pay attention in class.

The residents of Cancerland

In the meantime, you can stop the philosophising as you have a busy life to live. As a newly admitted member of the coolest posse on the planet, the cancer elite, you get to move fluidly and easily in interesting circles. Getting to know the residents is one of the pleasures of living in Cancerland. Starting at the top, the aristos and long-term residents:

Katherine L is a very high-status Liver, with multiple metastases – or 'Mets', as we residents know to call them now. She is in effect the Duchess of Cancerland. She is my age, has her routine, her court, knows every hospital, every consultant, has beautiful eyes with a touch of weariness underneath them, a radiant smile and since her diagnosis on Christmas Eve 2009, has been living as a dual citizen of London and Cancerland. "I live in a parallel world," as she put it. She has been through the whole gamut of treatments, and is now on nuclear therapy, which is as extreme and exotic as it sounds: you don't get higher status than that. We agree that, while it is lovely to be told you are brave, bravery is really about choosing to do something frightening that you don't have to do. Dealing with cancer is not being brave as you have no choice – it is more like having a full-time job than anything else. Katherine likes my concept of being a dual citizen. "Yes, that is exactly it, but I spend much more time in Cancerland than anywhere else."

We met at the 80th birthday party of Auntie Licky, a much loved Romanian-Jewish aunt, an honorific rather than blood relation – my grandmother and her mother had been best friends in pre-war Mittel-Europa. Auntie Licky's family had fled Hitler eastwards, through Romania, Bulgaria and Turkey to Palestine, then later, to London. My mother's family had fled westwards to British Columbia.

"What are *you* doing here?" Katherine asked me, raising an imperial eyebrow.

"I am here for Auntie Licky," I said. "What are *you* doing here?"

"She's not *your* Auntie Licky," Katherine replied, a trifle territorially, "or we would be related, as she is *my* Auntie Licky."

We had a brief and heated argument about whose Auntie Licky Auntie Licky was. Which we took to Auntie Licky herself to adjudicate.

"Dahlinks, I love you both, I am both your Auntie Licky," said Auntie Licky.

Auntie Licky died aged 90, and Katherine and I met again at the funeral. We had both just started a new round of chemo, so sat and talked shop, surrounded by the cosy and familiar European Jewish chatter of a warm and chaotic diaspora family. Older ones explain to younger ones how they are third cousins once removed as their great-aunts Fina, Fifi and Tutsi were sisters/first cousins – "except for you, Ileana," says Katherine pointedly, "you are not really related…" Then they all contradict each other. There was a family tree, but Auntie Licky had said that it was all wrong, so no one knew anything anymore. Then they try to fit in a whole raft of elderly male relatives, all called Bobby or Bubby or Bubberli. "Bobby was my uncle"/"No, that was Bubbi"/"No, Bobby and Bubbi just mean boy in Yiddish – they were all called Bubbi."

"What about Uncle Bubbily?

"That is just what Bubbi was called in Romania, the non-Jews thought it was his real name."

"So what was his name?"

"Adrian."

"But that was the other Uncle Bubbi's name."

"Yes, he was also called Adrian."

Auntie Licky's nickname was the "Late Licky", because she was always late for everything. At the cemetery, it turned out that her super-organised son Robert (named after his father Bubby) had forgotten the burial licence, so had to dispatch his wife to get it, which held things up for a good hour. "Licky is late again," as someone observed. "The late, late Licky."

Katherine's husband threw a surprise birthday party for her not long ago, but sadly she was hospitalised the day before and the party was called off. She wrote to me afterwards, "If the Duchess doesn't make her own party because she is in hospital, does that elevate her to Princess?" She is getting the hang of it, I am glad to see, and my concept is catching on.

If there is a sea change in how high-status cancer patients view their situation as a result of my ranking system, I will modestly accept credit.

Gerald F is a tall, elegant Old Etonian Liver Metastasis with snapping blue eyes. He used to be an officer in the Gurkhas, was a mountain guide in Nepal, speaks Sikkimese, Bahasa and Hindi, and now directs eye-watering sums of Asian money into European real estate projects. "Do you go back to India much?" I ask him over a herbal tea one day.

"Ah, not really, bit of a long story. I don't think they would be very keen on having me back," he drawls. "Got into a spot of bother last time, you know... they probably wouldn't let me in – or out again..."

Echoes of the North-West Frontier float around him like wisps of fog, and the pin-sharp suit and tie dissolve into epaulettes, sashes and frogging. We are supposed to be having a business meeting but we are much more interested in comparing our cancers. Gerald did not get on with his oncologist, stopped all treatment and for the last five years has been going once a year to a doctor in Germany who believes in dietary-based immunotherapy. "It is a very nice diet," says Gerald encouragingly to me. "You can have all the wine and coffee and cheese you want," here he looks with distaste at my herbal tea, "you just have to give up meat and sugar."

Gerald didn't tell anyone he had cancer, only a few friends. He still hasn't. This is a man thing. "Don't want any fuss," was Gerald's laconic answer to my bewildered "But why ever not tell anyone?"

Women tell everyone, garner sympathy, special treatment, little presents, treats and flowers and justify hitting the summer sales. Men don't; if they lose their hair, no one notices anyway, so in that sense, they can get away with it easier, but still.

Peter B is a travel journalist and we go way back. Amazingly we not only both have cancer and are doing chemotherapy, but we recently both turned up at the same time on the same small Greek island, missing each other by five minutes at a little outdoor party in a bunting-hung village square outside a small church. "Come and have supper with me!" I texted him the next day. "I can't, I am too busy vomiting." We understand each other perfectly.

Susie J is a 65-year-old, very high-status Metastatic Melanoma. She is so high status that she and half her family have moved to Texas for six months to be treated in one of those US clinics that are the only ones in the world to offer any hope. The costs are totally unregulated, the treatment brutal, the guarantees non-existent, and her 95-year-old mother, who is sharp as a tack and drives herself around to her various hobby and social events and is always immaculately dressed, charming and full of stories, has been busy taking out a mortgage on her house to pay for it all, with an acumen and efficiency that I can only dream of. "I got very good interest rates and it all takes effect in a week." The mother escaped from Hitler's Vienna to England as a child, on one of the Kindertransport trains, so the uncomplaining energy that she throws into this unexpected twist to her life, when she could be forgiven for thinking that she was home and dry after the storms of earlier years, is one of the most remarkable things I have ever come across. When I tell her this, she just says, "Nonsense, I am old and useless."

Alexander S is a Recovering Colon. Not really a resident in fact… a tourist. His wife, a gentle and soft soul whose body has not been deformed by any nasty masculine muscles since she was born, has taken up the gym in the hope that he will be encouraged to join in. So far she has developed great abs, can run up a hill without getting out of breath, row, skip, jump, crunch, lunge, plank, cycle, do burpies, warrior poses,

sun salutations and downward dogs, while Alex watches
her admiringly from the sofa with a brandy in hand. Soon,
she will be stronger than him which will be interesting. I
showed him this paragraph when I last saw him. He read
silently with an impassive expression that did not bode well
for our relationship. "Do you like it?" I asked timidly.

"No," he replied. "I don't."

"Why not?" I persevered.

"First, I don't drink brandy, I drink gin or whisky.
Second, it is all about Maria and not about me at all."

Charlotte P had breast cancer a few years ago, but didn't
tell anyone in her family about it as they would then make
her have chemo and radiation, and at 70, she really couldn't
be bothered with all of that. She is very pious, trusts in
Jesus, and since she had to give up champagne and cigarettes for health problems a few years before, she really is
not too fussed about dying, which luckily she shows no sign
of doing at all.

Shirley works on a cancer ward giving massage therapies to
patients. She tells me how many older women she sees who
by the time they are in their seventies really have no objec-
tion to dying: their lives have been lived, things will only
get worse, and truly, they would much rather not have the
chemo and all the rest; but their family make them do it.
"What can I do?" they say resignedly and miserably.

When my mother's cancer metastasised to her liver it wasn't
caught until it was pretty well terminal. My father had died
a few years before, and she said to us all and to Dr H with

great firmness that she didn't want to have treatment. She wouldn't have minded living longer, she said, but to go through horrible treatment for the sake of a few years was not something she would choose. Dr H told us it would all be over then in six weeks. We all moved home with our small children, and six weeks later, to the day, she died very peacefully in bed at two in the morning. We opened a bottle of champagne to toast her.

Her last words were "Ileana, don't forget to have the curtains mended in the guest room, don't let Marina [my older sister] have anything that needs folding or can break, and look after Paola [my younger sister]." Her presence hung around the house for a good few months, checking the curtains had been mended, telling me I was putting too much salt in the cooking, until it was OK for her to retire. A life well lived and well ended. When people say that I am being so brave, I say I really am not, this is the norm for me. I have never been a weeper and wailer and wouldn't know how to start doing that now, or deal with weepers and wailers myself.

There are, as well as the aristocrats of Cancerland, the usual annoying officials and jobsworths that you find in any country. Trying to get my subscription for sleeping pills renewed – I found that suddenly the dose had been reduced by half, as well as the number of pills, with the advice to take them only twice a week – I rang the surgery to be told that the prescribing doctor wasn't sure why I had been given sleeping pills to start with as they were a controlled substance that could make you sleepy. *They weren't sure why I had been prescribed them??*

"What do you mean why?" I snapped at the receptionist,

"I have stage 4 cancer of the liver, chemically induced meno-pause, a husband who snores, and I'm doing chemo for the second year in a row which fills me with sleep-disrupting drugs and gives me cramps and other side-effects – what more do I have to have wrong with me for me to get sleeping pills? Do they think that a *sleeping pill addiction* is what I am going to die of?" I waited gleefully for the doctor to call me back so I could remind him what chemo-tongue is like. He didn't, of course, so I had to meekly make an appoint-ment with the next available doctor in ten days' time, who turned out to be a charming girl who asked me how many pills I was short – it turned out that maths was not a strong point for either of us – we arrived at the number 21, prob-ably as it was the sum total of both our sets of fingers plus one for luck.

The cancer clear-out

As people realise you are moving to Cancerland, you'll find the dynamics of your friendships may change and shift, some fading away altogether. Some people simply feel awkward around cancer, not knowing how to behave or what you might want from them – this, in spite of your useful list of bullet-point tips called *Things not to say to a cancer patient* (see page 119). Some people, not always the ones you expect, step right up and become very close to you. They are comfortable with you, with your new nationality, the new language, the mores and customs of the country. Others discreetly disap-pear – no hard feelings – you might have been one of those yourself. Life becomes full of surprises.

There are material casualties of cancer as well. Cancer, as mentioned earlier, resembles pregnancy; just as expecting mothers start spring-cleaning in preparation for the great event, for three or four days around chemo, depending on the level of steroids you are on, you feel the urgent need to clean your house, rearrange furniture, chuck out rubbish, and stockpile loo paper. A sort of battening down the hatches in readiness for the chemo storm where you can't do anything for days afterwards. I have always loved chucking things out anyway; nothing makes my heart sing as much as hiring a skip and filling it up. My family post spies to watch me when this frenzy takes me as I do not limit my chucking-out to my own things. Like a hurricane, I whirl around the house, sucking up any loose objects off shelves, tables, window-sills, desks and floors, and depositing them in black rubbish bags. Then I go into drawers and boxes. Sometimes I chuck out the drawers and boxes without even opening them. It makes not a dent in the amount of stuff in the house, so I don't know why everyone gets upset.

My husband has taken to hoarding all his belongings in his study which is his "safe space" into which I am not allowed to whirl. Even the cleaning lady is not allowed in there. Just him, the three dogs, their baskets, his files, crates of wine, golf clubs, old shoes, hunting trophies, boxes of ammunition, old magazines, bridge manuals, frame-less pictures, sea-shells, pebbles, loose photos, binoculars, mangoes, jam jars of coins, and deeper layers that I haven't yet explored.

For a while there were even sacks of chicken feed, which he kept for years after the fox had eaten the last chicken, and I had to throw it out when he was away on a business trip as the sacks had started squeaking and rustling and wriggling, and when I opened one to see what was going on, thousands of maggots made their bid for freedom.

My younger, eco-warrior son goes through the rubbish to stop me throwing away things that should be recycled. He retrieves old vacuum cleaners, burnt saucepans, broken phone chargers and printers, and then leaves them outside the house for months as he is sadly too busy at work to actually recycle them. I then throw them all away again, he re-retrieves them, and they spend another couple of months in the rain outside the house and so on ad infinitum.

My daughter, on the other hand, not only possesses more stuff than the rest of the family put together, but has an eidetic memory for any object, whomsoever it belongs to. She goes through the rubbish regularly, rescuing loose beads, old batteries, single earrings, bottle tops, postcards, plastic curtain rings, mouldy photo albums, all of which seem to have some mysterious sentimental value, and brings me objects, quivering all over with tearful outrage: "How could you throw this away? It is the ashtray that someone gave me on my 15th birthday and which broke the day after so I could never use it."/"This tiny plastic elephant was part of a set of 12 and is the only one left since your last clear-out."

Having cancer-nesting syndrome amplifies this tendency of mine. So, before Chemo Round Two starts, the skip is ordered; the family put on notice to hide anything they particularly value, and sagging sofas, wormy chairs, rib-less umbrellas, suitcases full of spiders, pots, photo albums, boxes of letters, ping-pong nets, odd crutches, paddling pools with holes, a garden bench with no legs, a rusted trampoline, toasters, juicers, garlic crushers, broken deck-chairs, fondue sets, steam-cleaners, courgetti-spiralisers, Magimix accessories, files and filing cabinets, extension cables, wok-lids, cocktail-shakers, spare door-handles, gold-sprayed pine-cones, pots of paint, bathroom tiles, mop-heads, feather duster handles, bicycle helmets, old curtains, sewing-machines, string-less guitars, black and white art books, videos and record collections, will all be glee-fully winging their way into the skip in a veritable orgy of throwing-out. Now no one can say anything to stop me as I have cancer and everyone and everything is disposable… especially when a skip is squatting happily in the drive. Not everyone has a place in Cancerland, and there is certainly no room for all their *stuff*.

Ay de mi!! Tengo cáncer!! Mi amor,
adios para siempre!!

Chemo television review, part II
Sadly, *The Big Bang Theory* and *Two and a Half Men* can only be watched, even by one as addicted as me, a certain number of times, so my patient and inventive daughter has set up a brand new iPad for me as an entertainment centre – with my music irretrievably muddled up, non-alphabeti-cally by iTunes' latest "update for your convenience" (thank you so much, iTunes), but more brilliantly, with a whole new universe of *telenovelas* stored on it.

Jane the Virgin (series 1-5) will see me through countless otherwise dull chemo-hours and insomniac nights, and my Spanish is already coming on in leaps and bounds. As the same Latino actors also appear in *Devious Housemaids* but in different roles, there is a certain post-modernist deconstructivism to my viewing that means I am totally on trend. My paper will be coming up soon – "Bilingual commentaries on identity fluidity in bi-cultural societies in North and Central America".

Podcasts are another revelation: great for insomnia. *Shit Town* got me through many sleepless nights; *My Dad wrote a Porno* got me though one no-mates chemo session where the TLC failed to show up – I sobbed so loudly with laughter on the day I listened to it that the nurse came running in to offer me Counselling. They had never had anyone crying with laughter in cubicle number 2 before…

The only problem with podcasts is that I find myself getting hard of hearing in a very dowager-duchessy sort of way: chemo-hearing, of course – how did I not spot that one last time round? The main sound to fall victim to this deafness is American accents. *The Serial*, a very fine US podcast that investigates miscarriages of justice, is almost ruined for me by the fact that the narrator, a clearly brilliant, sympathetic, original, thoughtful and probably beautiful girl, is barely comprehensible. She elides her words so that "This year" becomes "Thih zyeer". A whole sentence might be "Thih zyeer, wye lye wah zgoing to the cor troo moh stays, ahrealye zthah twat ever happen, die wooh dnever know the truth."

"Sarah, love," I wanted to shout, "Sarah, love, speak properly for heaven's sake!!"

Adding to the feeling of being an elderly dowager is the annoyance of a badly fitting temporary bridge following the extraction of a perfectly good tooth in preparation for taking Zometa and avoiding necrotising jaw disease. Together with the aching joints, deafness, blindness and hair loss, the temporary bridge makes s's and other sibilants now whistle and bubble sideways into my cheek as I talk, so in fact, what I would have shouted to Sarah would have been more like, "Sharah, love, shpeak properly for heavensh shake!"

A recent conversation on the phone with a girlfriend who had lost a tooth in a riding accident and was also whistling through her badly fitting temporary bridge went like this.

Cathryn: "I 'ahn't talk 'roperly azh I 'av a oof infecshu.'"

Me: "Shoundzh ghashtly, I am sho shorry."

I asked a friend of mine who had had lots of chemo if she too experienced chemo-hearing, but she told me that she has been deaf in one ear from childhood, so couldn't tell. In fact, what she said rather loudly was, "What?" – until I had repeated it a couple of times into her good ear.

Wedding anniversaries

We have never celebrated these before – mainly because we both forget the date – but we are also not very comfortable with scheduled emotions. Valentine's Day has always been studiously ignored, while birthdays are allowed as it is all about *me* rather than about love and other soppy things.

This year, though, was our 30th wedding anniversary, which really is an achievement, and for which we managed to be on our small island in Greece where we had got married. The words "*for better for worse, for richer for poorer, in sickness and health, till death us do part*" take on a special resonance now. As I mentioned, my husband and I have furious arguments over who gets to die first and who has to bury whom and live on their own afterwards. We are both deadly serious and I am winning, though there is never any room for complacency.

Our wedding ceremony had taken place in 100 degrees heat. The men's collars were all curling up in the humidity, while I had surreptitiously cut off the gauze petticoats of my dress and removed my shoes, which were just white satin puddles of sweat. The priest, in his layers of black serge, with the sweat dripping down his face, gabbled as fast as he could so we could all leave the stifling church and go and get ice cream from the village shop across the square. As the ceremony was in Old Church Greek, I don't think anyone actually said, "in sickness and in health, etc., etc.", and even if they did, we wouldn't have understood them. My German husband's Greek is limited to "more wine please" while my Old Church Greek is patchy at best. The Greek wedding ceremony is more like, "God says stay together and don't fool around, but if you do fool around, you can marry up to two more times in church before I say *enough*." Or *"Vayase para siempre"* perhaps. Pragmatism is a Greek word, while romance and fidelity are Latin ones, though as idealism, asceticism and dogma are also Greek, I don't really know where I am going with this. It seemed promising when I started the sentence.

I did once hire a Greek teacher for my husband – a very beautiful and intelligent girl called Katerina, with a voluptuous bosom, masses of black hair and flashing teeth and eyes – she was definitely over-qualified in all respects. Ancient Greek roots freely sailed past my husband's intellectual horizon, undetained by any mental grappling hooks, and I was only allowed in at half time to serve coffee (Greek, one spoon of sugar). After a year, he had learned to say, "My name is Florian", so we discontinued the lessons although we finally all knew what his name was. Katerina left for America where she has become a very popular professor of modern Greek culture at Loyola University in Los Angeles, and Florian has added "I want a boiled egg, please" to his Greek vocabulary.

At breakfast under an olive tree on the day of our anniversary, a huge bouquet of 30 red roses lay on the table. Impressed, as I didn't think the Greek village florist did red roses, I asked our housekeeper who had sent them. "Guess," she said. I started guessing, starting with the local mayor, then going down the whole list of people I knew in the village, before trying extended family and friends. Then I gave up. "Who?" "Your husband of course."

Perhaps he emailed Katerina and learned "*Trianda kokkina triandafila.*" It is wonderful that after 30 years, you can still be surprised by your spouse. We went to a small taverna in the hills for dinner and feasted on very local kid, succulent with lemon and oregano, to the sound of goat bells and touchingly unsuspecting and contented bleating from the rustling bushes nearby, while the stars started peeping out of a velvet sky.

Green planet

Encouraged by my efforts at green juicing last summer, my daughter, who has the greenest fingers ever to sprout from a human palm, has planted a vegetable garden. Terrifying quantities of kale, rainbow chard and unidentified green things, which should have been lettuce but grow like the rain forest, continuously burst forth from the ground. These leaves are so ferociously bitter and medicinal that the slugs won't touch them, nor will the birds and certainly no one else in the family, not even the eco-warrior son. So I look at the Amazonian green stretching endlessly before me, mournfully pick a sackful of chlorophyll, which makes not the slightest dent in the massed rows, and then wander back to the kitchen for a chocolate biscuit. Well-meaning nutritionists from the clinic email me to invite me to "Eating Well" courses. I should really invite the whole class over to my daughter's vegetable patch. I did tell one of the dieticians that my current diet consisted of bitter garden spinach and chard, chicken livers cooked in vodka, paprika, sour cream and chocolate biscuits. "Ooh," she cooed innocently, "I am very fond of spinach…"

So that is one I can count on.

Practice makes perfect

Losing your hair again after it has only just grown back a bit – child's play, you hardly notice. In fact you sometimes forget and answer the door bare-headed which is frightening for other people. Plus, you already have all the turbans, though there will always be room for the latest Missoni – which happens to have gold lamé in it, so has already been ordered.

While last time the hair you lost was long and lustrous

and easily identifiable as yours, this time, the hairs falling out are short and look exactly like dog hairs, with the result that after you have sat somewhere, people sigh in annoyance, brush off the cushions or pillows and shoo the dogs away, all three of whom then look at you reproachfully as they know perfectly well it was you.

The Tuesday Lunch Club swings back into action.

Waiting rooms – nah ah – not for VIPs; you just walk up to the chemo suite unannounced, and they know which "your" chair is – the one with the most natural light and a good view of what is going on.

Ultrasounds – you know which medical centres provide heated gel and make snide comments about the centres that don't. You also brief each imaging doctor before you start – "You would be surprised," said Dr P darkly to me one day, "how long I sometimes spend looking for people's gall bladders, and then they say – 'oh, sorry, I forgot to say, I had it removed a few years ago…'"

PET scans and MRIs – you know to make sure the microphones are working before the nurses leave the room and to tell them to let you know exactly how long each segment of different clanging and clanking is going to last. And you have at last prepared your music requests. With my Chill Jazz Lounge playlist specially bookmarked, I actually fell asleep in my last PET scan, which is the holy grail of all scannees, while Randy Crawford gently bewailed the rain that night in Georgia.

Self-defence techniques – people want to hug you to show you how much they care, which is lovely, but you probably have a chestful of scars and chemo ports, so you learn to take subtle avoidance measures, including slipping your arm up to your breast to cushion the hug-impact without anyone noticing.

And yes!!! Finally, the Oncology Physiotherapist tells you that push-ups and planks are BAD for those of us who have no lymph glands. "No more of those," she says sternly. "I promise," you say happily.

Insurance

Getting your German insurer's letters of guarantee out to all the various independently run clinics where you have your scans, X-rays, consultant appointments, blood tests and surgeries is a skill in itself, and one I happily leave to my husband who feels he could open a consultancy on the intricacies. He could certainly help with bi-lateral Anglo-German Brexit negotiations, which call for the harmonising of two incompatible systems and a feel for what both Brits and Germans respond to.

I had in fact missed a unique opportunity to place myself close to the seat of power here. Florian never allowed me anywhere near his business contacts after he caught me once explaining to a financial regulator over a business lunch that I saw nothing wrong with insider trading. He leaned across me to the startled man, explained smoothly that I was "a Levantine", and never took me anywhere again.

Years later, he agreed to give me a second chance, and

allowed me to come to a particularly stuffy business dinner. I was seated next to a balding Swedish man who, unusually, also managed to have a light cover of dandruff on his shoulders. He worked at the European Commission, chairing a feasibility study on how to harmonise different national insurance company policies. I saw it as my chance of redemption in my husband's eyes, and made it my business to be as charming as I could. No woman had ever shown such interest in, or grasp of, the differences between Belgian and Luxembourgish insurance regulations. No woman had ever fluttered her eyelashes as alluringly at the mention of "cross-border provisional focus group studies". No woman had ever asked such penetratingly intelligent questions about Scandinavian medical code systems or listened in such open-mouthed admiration to the answers. By the time dessert was served, the Swedish insurance harmoniser leaned towards me, dropped his voice to a whisper, and said, "I must see you again, please let me have your telephone number so I can call you when I am in London for the next meeting of the European Commission departmental cross-border insurance workshop."

On the way home, I told this to my husband proudly, expecting praise and admiration. It was the last time he ever asked me to accompany him on a business dinner. Most ungrateful.

I now wonder if I should have given the Swede my real telephone number instead of a fake one; I would now be in a position, 20 years later, to explain directly to Sven, my best friend, the big cheese of the European Commission, precisely where the difficulties lie in harmonising the various national insurance regulations.

Sparkling conversation

Apart from the three days around chemo when you are strung out on steroids, undergoing chemotherapy is not likely to be your time to sparkle at social gatherings. Some people find that they avoid going out, not because they don't feel well enough, but because they dread the moment when the person they are talking to asks them what they do and they have to reply that they used to be an x, y or z, but now have cancer so are not doing very much.

Women find it harder to hide their cancer because baldness and discoloured fingernails are more obvious on women than men. So, we tend to prefer saying we have cancer rather than to let people think we are just plain ugly and unkempt. This can be a real conversation-killer and the interlocutor, especially if English, sits silently, covered in embarrassment and unable to find anything else to say.

There are various ways to control these situations. I found being able to say that I was writing a book very helpful. It is not as if anyone is interested, and you don't even actually have to be writing anything at all; what it means is that they can tell you about *their* book, which a surprising number of people have somewhere on a back burner, and of course is of great interest, sometimes even to you, and this will see you safely through to shore.

The chances are that the person you are speaking to will also have a friend, relative or colleague with cancer, or may even have had it him or herself, so that gives you lots and lots to talk about. You can also use it *in extremis* as an ice-breaker; I was at an event where a man was making a simply interminable speech. Not only was it interminable, but the microphone wasn't working properly and we couldn't hear it at our end of the room. After 20 minutes or so, some of us gave up and started whispering to each other, and at one point, our chat might have got a bit too loud. The man at the end of the table leaned over to me and said severely, "Do be quiet, the speaker is still talking, wait till he has finished."

I shot right back at him, "I have stage 4 cancer of the liver and I am not sure I am going to live that long."

To my horror, he put his head down on the table and started sobbing. I touched his arm to see if he was alright, and he turned his head sideways while still leaving it on the table, and said with tears in his eyes, "That is just about the funniest thing I have ever heard!" I then saw that he was crying with laughter.

Cancer is of course a wonderful excuse to get out of anything you don't want to do, but there is no need to stay home worrying on the grounds that you will be a party-pooper.

Physiotherapy

I wish I had asked for this much earlier – more than a year since surgery, and I still couldn't lie on my tummy. Louise sees me once a fortnight to try to break up the scar tissue. Physio-terrorism she calls it.

One day we were interrupted by a fire drill and the building, which is full of sophisticated, highly combustible machinery, was evacuated. We stood for a while in the road while the receptionists donned fire-marshal, high-vis jackets and created pandemonium shepherding people in the wrong direction; then Louise said, "Let's go over to the mothership in Harley Street and see if they have a room for us."

The receptionist there looked a bit startled to be confronted by two women asking for a room for half an hour where they could have some privacy. She was a trouper, though, studied her book and then said, "You could have the board-room, that is all I can offer you, I am afraid."

"Ooh, yes, Louise, please let's, we have never done it in a board-room before!" I said, before realising how bad it sounded. The row of men in the waiting room looked at us half-scandalised, half-hopeful.

"No," said Louise severely, "we can't do it in the board-room, we need a proper bed. We will go over to the chemo suites and use the recliner chairs there." Feeling the eyes of the waiting room upon us, there was nothing for it but to brazen it out. I put my arm around Louise's waist and we sauntered out as demurely as we could.

The recliner chair in the chemo suite – with the curtains drawn – was just fine.

Roller coaster

Just the fact that Prof E had told me that only a tiny percentage of Metastases can be cured, while the others all have to be managed brought the competitive streak out in me again. The old Ileana whispered, "You can do it!" The new and wiser Ileana whispered back, "You probably can't and *it doesn't matter either!*"

I have reacted to everything in an extreme way – I

tolerated chemo unusually well, my test results all shone brilliantly, but on the other hand, I metastasised faster than anyone would have believed possible, and also managed to change my cancer type in doing so, which is exceptionally rare. After I finally finished with the second lot of chemo, I was scanned to see what the results were. To everyone's amazement, my school reports were good again, top of the class. There was no sign of any cancer activity and about 90% of the cancer cells seemed to have disappeared. Those who took Science Ed 1 will understand that this means that any cancer cells still lying around had been blown up, killed, put to sleep, or had all their receptors broken off. In almost record time, I was now officially "in remission".

"Fascinating," said Prof E yet again when I met him to discuss this. "We might prolong the chemo as it doesn't seem to bother you, and we could aim for getting rid of those last 10% of cancer cells, even though they seem to have been switched off, though sometimes," here he paused, "too much chemo can teach the cells to mutate and it all goes wrong again…" I can tell that he is going to ask my opinion on what to do quite soon, as he has forgotten that I am a Libra, so I head him off and tell him not to get too excited as, given my exceptional track record, I will probably re-metastasise faster than anyone else, with yet another mutation – on my roller coaster, anything could happen.

I admit that, even though I had moderated my ambition and expectations, the thought that I am very likely to last much longer than five years meant that I couldn't help but go shopping; not for frivolous nonsense which is for those with a decidedly short life-span ahead of them, but celebration shopping for cashmere and timeless classics that will never go out of fashion, will last for years, and suit you when you are much older; the best kind of shopping.

Remission

The day Prof E told me that I was officially in remission and we could stop the chemo, even though I was expecting him to say it, was unexpectedly moving, even for me who am determinedly unmoved by anything at all. I would have shed a couple of tears of happiness if only to please Prof E who was clearly ecstatic, had both my eyes, which normally flowed like the Niagara Falls, not been crusted and gummed up with conjunctivitis – another chemo side-effect. I couldn't even drum up a little moist gleam or shine.

I hoped he wasn't disappointed at my reaction. Remission means that the cancer cells, which are undoubtedly some-where inside you, have been battered into submission, lost their mojo, and are dormant. They have been rehabilitated, have joined a knitting club and take old ladies ballroom dancing at tea-time. The idea is to keep them in that state for ever. Every three weeks from now on I am to have what is fondly known as an "infusion" to make it sound more fragrant and delicate than it really is. This is just like chemo but without the carpet-bombing toxic stuff, just guided missiles targeting the cell receptors – the pencils stuck in the fist – and something to wipe out any foolish oestrogen hormones optimistically trying to make a guest appear-ance. One of the three "infusion" elements is Zometa, definitely neither fragrant nor delicate, in spite of having a pretty name, and reduces you to bed-rest and mega doses of Ibuprofen for two days, which I should have guessed from the fact that I had to sign a consent form. One never learns. I am assured that this effect will wear off as I get used to it. If it doesn't, I will tell Prof E where he can infuse his Zometa…

In fact, I did try to tell Prof E where he could infuse his Zometa; plucking up my courage, I made an appointment to tell him that it was horrid and I didn't want to have it any more. "OK," he said straight away. "We can drop it. You don't really need it, it isn't absolutely essential."

A cancer cell in remission

I was expecting a battle that I would lose, and my intention was just to have a little whine, not do myself out of a life-saving drug, so this threw me. "But Prof," I said a trifle pathetically, "don't let me talk you out of giving me a drug that I might need, it isn't *that* horrid."

"No, no, we can drop it."

I was starting to panic now. "I was exaggerating really, it isn't too bad at all, perhaps I should have it to be safe?"

"It is fine, we can drop it."

"But if you think it is good for me, I really don't mind it!"

"It really isn't necessary, it was just a safety play."

This threw me into even more of a panic – "I want my Zometa!" I almost wailed. "Please, I didn't mean it, I am sorry!"

Prof E sighed, "We can always add it in later if we want but we are dropping it now."

Prof E ought to know by now not to listen to anything I say. And I ought to know that I should hold my tongue.

My life is now to be arranged in three-week blocks which you are not supposed to call chemo as it upsets everyone who loves you. There is no end in sight to this, which in Cancerland is good news. We call it a "light maintenance programme" and hope for it to go on for as long as possible. I have never wanted to disappear to the South Pacific for six months, or give it all up and open a beach bar in the Caribbean, but now, suddenly, I do, just because I can't. I am tied with an umbilical cord to Harley Street or its outposts for the rest of my hopefully long and happy life. I started to fill out my diary with every third Thursday at Harley Street, till I got to December 2023 and realised that

I was rather overdoing the organisation bit.

The diet thing is a bit depressing; a new and healthy daily routine now becomes imperative – the excuse that one is having chemo no longer works, and one really does have to deprive the remaining cancer cells of easy access to their favourite fuel: sugar.

In a serious attempt to give up chocolate biscuits at four o'clock, I decided to give up tea, into which chocolate biscuits obviously have to be dunked. What I overlooked is the fact that something nice needs to happen instead at four o'clock, so I have taken up drinking coffee, which I never used to do. Unfortunately, dunking a carrot stick in coffee is no better than dunking it in tea, so this has not solved the chocolate biscuit problem, but rather, has led to a coffee problem as well as a chocolate biscuit problem. Still, I have lots of time to get this right, so the situation remains fluid, so to speak.

Clinical trials

Miracles do happen; a recent study has revealed that asparagine, a substance found in asparagus, broccoli, kale and green vegetables, is suspected of actually *encouraging* cancer metastasis – in a petrie dish at least. Don't panic and stop eating your green vegetables yet; trials will shortly be under way. I cut this article out and took it to my next appointment with Prof E.

"Please," I said, "I want to go on a trial for drugs one can take to counteract the asparagine in green vegetables."

"You don't like taking the drugs that I *do* already

prescribe you," he said, with the tiniest sign of impatience. "Why do you want to take more drugs, especially ones that haven't even been trialled yet?" He had a point.

I muttered something feeble about being picky about my drugs.

He sighed. "Call this number and make an appointment at the clinical trial institute, and see what trials they have going there."

I guessed that, like a cat bringing dead mice to their owner's living room, I had brought him one too many newspaper articles, and he was kicking me upstairs, so to speak. Or outdoors through the cat-flap.

As I headed for Prof E's door, I saw the lady waiting for her appointment with him pick up the asparagine article I had left on the table. She read it, stared into space for a second, then marched with it into Prof E's room. I felt a guilty twinge, and left as quickly and quietly as I could.

I duly turned up at the clinical trial institute, armed with my folder of yellow highlighted print-outs. The doctor was the most drop-dead gorgeous glamour-puss I had ever seen, with long eyelashes, loads of hair (yes, I am still sensitive about that) and a husky Spanish accent. What with that and her Rita Heyworth looks, I am sure no one ever listens to anything she says. Her beauty removed all her credibility as a doctor, even though she was wearing what seemed to be stage-prop spectacles in an attempt to make people take her seriously. It goes to show that looks do not always help people in their career. She must have fought "lookism" all her life.

She pointed out to me that since I was on the right medication and was in remission, there was no point putting me on a trial. I could just imagine Prof E's grin, but luckily, she did add very sweetly that there was a "bery cool" trial coming up of an improved version of a drug I was already on, so I could be listed for that when the time came. She also directed me to a documentary that she said was called "Kill Yourself", on positive thinking and pain relief. I looked it up, and it turned out to be called "Heal Yourself", which made more sense.

I shall continue to bring Prof E dead mice whenever I catch them. It is such a great tease and you never know if something fun will come of it. I really get cats now.

In summary, the prognosis is good, though as even Pollyanna might secretly think, the downside is that I might last long enough to get Alzheimer's... For those of us with PPD, that is one reason to be glad, if things don't work out that well.

It is perhaps a little disappointing even for me to realise how shallow I am. Part One of this book, where I was not faced with thoughts of mortality or larger issues, ended with some profound thoughts on the meaning of life, whereas Part Two, where I am certainly facing the Big Issues, ends with no such pearls of wisdom. Perhaps profundity is over-rated. I once read a pleasingly down-to-earth definition of the meaning of life: pleasing in its total philosophical uselessness.

"The purpose of life is to hydrogenate carbon dioxide," wrote Michael Russell, a geochemist at Caltech, which in lay terms means, of course, "Go shopping" or some other similarly hydrogenating activity for carbon-based organisms like me; so perhaps I am on the right track after all. Caltech is the Alma Mater of *The Big Bang Theory* sitcom, so as far as I am concerned, is the fount of all wisdom and any proclamation emanating from its halls is to be received with silent reverence.

Living in Cancerland

Living in Cancerland turns out to be not unlike living anywhere really – just not in the fast lane. Your main job is of course maintaining your residency for as long as you can, but apart from that, life can go back to something very close to normal, at least something that looks like normal to the outside world. You know that you have an extra layer of experience, thoughts and emotions, rather like having an invisible friend who says good morning to you first thing, now and then makes the odd comment when you are not busy, and says good night to you; but a friend with whom you are perfectly comfortable living.

You understand that all the other Cancerland residents also live with their invisible friends, so really it can be quite a party. It turns out that my cruise ship sailed away and left me here on this continent, but it's OK. It has its beauties and monuments and a rich diversity of landscapes, you learn the language, you become a local, you make new friends, get used to the cuisine (just...) and your dearest and oldest friends all gladly come and visit and love you all the more.

Cancerland is not where you chose to live, but it is where your job has relocated, so you have to make the best of it. I have been lucky enough to move almost immediately to the very desirable, leafy residential quarter called Remission, from where I can do my monthly runs down to town for treatment, and from that peaceful vantage point, the views are good, the neighbours are lovely, I can commute easily between it and Normal-land, as can my family, and I am perfectly content to call it home for as long as I possibly can. My glass is always half full, and I raise it every day in silent gratitude for all my blessings.

Thanks

To Paul Ellis, Gerald Gui, Michael Harding and the team at the
LOC, without whom, quite literally, this book would
have been a lot shorter...

To Emma Sutcliffe, Lucy O'Donnell, John Gordon and Laura
Longrigg for their steadfast support and encouragement.

To the Tuesday Lunch Club – Kate, Emma, Andrew, Paula,
Mark, Marina, Ana, Ailsa, the Lauras, James, Rosie, Afreen,
Cristina and Mary for manfully pitching up to entertain me.
If I forgot anyone, please forgive me. Chemo-brain...

To Evie Dunne at Short Books for diplomatic editing of the
more tasteless of my stories and Aurea Carpenter for pretending
not to notice when I slipped back in all the bits she had cut out.

To Dr. Robert Möginger for keeping me so well insured.

Lastly, to family and friends for allowing themselves to be
written about, looking after me, and putting up with me.

Ileana von Hirsch is half Greek and half Hungarian, married to a Bavarian, has three children and too many dogs.

She has worked as a set designer and mural artist, has been in the travel business for 20 years and is hoping that cancer will give her an excuse to retire. The excellence of her medical care means that this is still a far-off dream.

Her feelings about writing a sequel to *A funny thing happened on the way to chemo* are mixed, as a boring life from now on is probably a good thing.